# MIRROR, MIRROR

## Transforming Narcissism to Self-Realization

Gayle Bohlman

 CHIRON PUBLICATIONS • ASHEVILLE, NORTH CAROLINA

Author Photo © Sandy Williams
Cover image from Pixabay

www.ChironPublications.com

Interior and cover design by Danijela Mijailovic
Printed primarily in the United States of America.

ISBN  978-1-63051-704-5 paperback
ISBN  978-1-63051-705-2 hardcover
ISBN  978-1-63051-706-9 electronic
ISBN  978-1-63051-707-6 limited edition paperback

Library of Congress Cataloging-in-Publication Data

Names: Bohlman, Gayle, author.
Title: Mirror, mirror : transforming narcissism to self-realization / by Gayle Bohlman.
Description: Asheville, N.C. : Chiron Publications, [2019] | Includes bibliographical references and index.
Identifiers: LCCN 2019020258 | ISBN 9781630517045 (pbk. : alk. paper) | ISBN 9781630517052 (hardcover : alk. paper)
Subjects: LCSH: Narcissism. | Self-realization.
Classification: LCC BF575.N35 B64 2019 | DDC 158.2--dc23
LC record available at https://lccn.loc.gov/2019020258

# Contents

The winged horse on the cover, Pegasus, symbolizes the emerging consciousness that has integrated the essence of the self, including its wounds, darkness, and the animating spirit that resides within. This powerful and beautiful image is a symbol of hope for the true self, which makes the journey to wholeness.

Dedicated
To my parents, Ethel and Irving

● ● ● ●

# Note to Reader

To be human is to experience wounds that disrupt or distort our connection to the Self. These are called narcissistic wounds and can result in narcissism that is visible as self-absorption and a lack of capacity for relatedness. It occurs in gradations along a continuum from healthy to pathological.

Healthy narcissism is self-advocating and protecting; pathological narcissism is a source of much pain for the narcissist and for those around him or her. Part of my motivation for writing this book is the looming presence of the narcissism seen in the current President of the United States, Donald Trump. This high visibility of narcissism offers a call to become more conscious of the dangers it holds and to recognize the necessity of healing the narcissism that impairs our individual and collective potential.

This is not a book about healing narcissistic personality disorder, which has a poor prognosis for change. Narcissism is, in fact, the opposite of self-realization and impedes our becoming all that we are capable of being. Self-realization is a process of coming to know the self. In Jungian psychology, the word *Self* is generally capitalized when referring to our full potential, the source of being which includes conscious and unconscious aspects. *Self* encompasses what we've experienced and also what we have not yet experienced but that also exists in the fulness of our being. So, Self with a capital S goes beyond the personal mind, body, and emotions to the transpersonal spirit. Jung understood Self as an archetype, implying a preexisting wholeness. This animating energy is a creation, not a construction, and thus may be understood as God within.

When I use the word *self* (lower case s), I'm speaking not of a concept but of a living, breathing presence, the core being that is both an experiential creature and an organizing principle at the center of the human being. This self is the personal aspect of the full potential of our being. It's what we know through our awareness of experience. Jung's non-dual understanding does not separate self from Self. Recovery from narcissism requires experiencing the true Self, the wholeness of being that resides within.

You will find here a depth exploration of narcissism and its recovery. As we join in understanding, preventing, healing, and transforming narcissism, we participate in the evolution of consciousness, which brings wholeness.

# Introduction

Now more than ever, humanity is tasked with healing the malady of narcissism. There are simply not enough problem-solving skills, political solutions, judicial remedies, or powers in the world to move us toward our true potential until we heal the narcissism within. As Donald Trump ascended to the presidency of the United States, those who elected him allowed a veil of denial to keep his narcissistic core out of their view.

Steven Buser suggests that the source of Trump's popularity may be a collective narcissistic complex: "Just as wounds create unconscious complexes within an individual, collective wounds sustained by a nation may cause cultural complexes within a nation's unconscious."[1] Such wounds to the collective psyche are brought about by events such as 9/11, the loss of jobs, and economic stagnation.

---

[1] Buser, S., & Cruz, L. (Eds.). (2017). *A Clear and Present Danger: Narcissism in the Era of President Trump*, p. 14. Asheville, NC: Chiron Publications.

"Make America Great Again" beckons to the shadow of wounding seeking comfort.

At this moment in history, we have the opportunity individually and collectively to look at our own shadows. In their book on narcissism, Steve Buser and Len Cruz comment, "The extreme utterances and behaviors displayed by candidates like Mr. Trump may have shined a light on narcissism and perhaps given society a chance to confront this phenomenon head-on."[2] The narcissistic wounds that this shadow holds and the transformation of this shadow material is essential to our individual and collective evolution.

Narcissism, according to the prevailing knowledge, has a poor prognosis for healing. All human beings are, to some degree, inherently self-absorbed. We are wired for survival, which requires vigilance about our safety and well-being. In addition, our sense of separateness as inhabitants of individual bodies promotes isolation, a disconnection from others, and a preoccupation with self-interest. When trapped in this sense of separateness, it is easy for selfishness to prevail.

Narcissism originates in core wounds that are usually unconscious and impenetrable. The psyche seeks to protect itself and so constructs defenses

---

[2] ibid, xi.

against the wounds to the true self, and these defenses constitute the foundation of narcissism.

*Complex*, a word originating in psychoanalytic theory, refers to an unconscious pattern that drives behavior. Complexes are formed out of experience, emotions, memories, and needs, and constellate around a theme. We speak of a superiority complex or a mother complex as patterns that exist around those themes that are unconscious. A complex may affect more than an individual. It might affect the environment or field in which it exists, and the environment may affect the complex.

In applying field theory to psychology, Jungian analyst Michael Conforti speaks of entire countries mobilized by an unconscious field. He uses Germany under Hitler as an illustration of the tremendous influence fields can have on a nation. "Through the embodiment of Hitler as leader, an entire country was moved to actions it would never have committed if it had not been possessed by powerful archetypal and unconscious content."[3]

Field theory examines the interaction between an individual or a particle of matter, and its environment. In physics, field theory is used to explain forces and relationships between particles. In psychology, it examines patterns of interaction between

---

[3] Conforti, M. (2003). *Field, Form, and Fate: Patterns in Mind, Nature, & Psyche*. New Orleans: Spring Journal Books.

the individual, the unconscious, and their environment. Jung created the term *archetype* to describe preexisting instinctive patterns in the unconscious that guide form and development. Jung saw Self, wholeness, king, scapegoat, mother, father, eternal child, and similar representations as archetypes. Conforti studied the fields in which archetypes and individual psyches interact. He says that field theory "postulates that matter is the outcome and not the source of the creative process,"[4] and quotes Gary Zukav: "Fields alone are real. They are the substance of the universe. Matter (particles) is simply the momentary manifestation of interacting fields, which intangible and insubstantial as they are, are the only real things in the universe."[5]

If we look into the shadow complex of the United States during this time as evidenced by Trump's appeal, what do we see? Tom Singer suggests that these characteristics dwell in that shadow:

A self-promoting brand

Arrogant bullies in our conduct of business and other relations

Very limited in our capacity for self-reflection

Filled with hubris and a lack of humility

---

[4] ibid, p. 50.
[5] Zukav, G. (2009). *Dancing Wu Li Masters: An Overview of the New Physics*, p. 219. San Francisco: HarperOne.

Self-absorbed with little sensitivity for the
needs of others

Possessed by greed and consumerism

So entitled in our good fortune that we have
come to believe this is our due[6]

The shadow may have created a field establishing
someone like Donald Trump as leader in this time.
This field brings forth someone like Trump as a visible
expression of itself in the environment. Because this
Trump event is atypically evident and preposterously
amplified, it calls our attention to the narcissistic
core wounds in the field of American society. Fortunately, not only does the field affect the individual
but the individual may affect the field. Thus, what
many see as a crisis is also an opportunity to raise
our consciousness and affect change in the field. To
have such an effect, we would do well to deepen our
understanding of narcissism.

Narcissism is essentially the opposite of our
human capacity for relatedness. A narcissist lacks
empathy for others, while relatedness grasps the
experience of others with compassion. Narcissism
pursues individual gain, relatedness seeks the good

---

[6] Singer, T. (2017). President Trump and the American selfie:
archetypal defenses of the group spirit. In S. Buser & L. Cruz, (Eds.).
*A Clear and Present Danger,* p. 50.

of the whole. Narcissism is driven by fear, relatedness is animated by love.

Narcissism exists because of wounds to the true self, and is sustained by a defensive structure unconsciously designed to prevent pain. This effort to prevent pain is inevitably unsuccessful. There remains a void at the core of the narcissist that is full of dark pain. Narcissism itself generates pain for others in its failures at relatedness.

Narcissism seems to run in families and research being conducted on the brain and its structures in this type of disorder is underway. Dr. James Fallon scanned the brains of psychopaths and observed that the limbic systems in these brains were turned off, that is, the capacity for empathy was missing.

In the course of his research, Fallon inadvertently discovered that his own brain is significantly similar to the brain of a psychopath, and his family history is consistent with this. After he broke through his own denial, he began to practice making behavioral changes that express more empathy, even though he had to do it with cognitive intention, rather than genuine emotional empathy. He says his wife appreciated the change even if it was cognitive rather than emotional.[7]

---

[7] Fallon, J. Neuroscientist. A scientist's journey through psychopathy. https://www.youtube.com/watch?v=lOjykLQAdaE on 2019-03-24

Changing one's brain is difficult. Behaviors become entrained and unconscious factors support repetition rather than modification. Recent research into neuroplasticity reveals the brain's potential for change throughout the life span, and epigenetics research has shown certain DNA instructions may be turned on or off through environmental and lifestyle changes. More research on the structure of the brain of those expressing narcissism will help our understanding of this condition and will help us consider ways to bring about change in spite of the brain's propensities and limitations.

Narcissism expresses in gradations. This book will be of most benefit to those with mild narcissism, whose wounds—with effort—can become conscious, allowing connection to the true self. As Cruz and Buser describe, "Most of us are simple garden-variety neurotics, which means we have erred, we suffer our disconnections, know we are at fault, and know we have to get back in line with some deeper principle within. This knowing represents our attenuated but still living thread to the Self."[8]

This is in stark contrast to the narcissist who believes there is nothing at all wrong with him or her. Awareness of that person's woundedness falls to others, since the narcissist cannot see or feel the wounds.

---

[8] Buser, S. & Cruz, L. (Eds.). (2017). *A Clear and Present Danger*, p. 8.

Severe narcissistic personality structures do not seem to maintain that "living thread to the Self."

I want to affirm the experience of many, that the narcissist in their life just won't change. This is a necessary recognition, lest one lose one's self in the darkness of the shadow that narcissism will cast on the lives of those in its circle. I had to come to that recognition in my own life and chose to save myself.

This book can help in understanding the underlying structure of narcissism in the psyche. It can help us recover the loss of connection to the true self, which we all experience to some extent. If you've been wounded by narcissism in your relationships, this book will help you discover a path of healing. In the hope that we can have less narcissism dominating our lives going forward, I'll describe what it takes to prevent the wounding from which narcissism arises and what is needed to break through some narcissistic defenses.

*Mirror, Mirror* offers insight into a healing process for narcissism through the exploration of three well-known myths. We begin with the fairy tale *Snow White*. This story helps us see that narcissism is a wound that must be understood for it to heal. *Snow White* also points to mirroring as the most important element of recovery.

The narcissist desperately seeks mirroring. Desperately. Mirroring is a critical element in child development as explained by attachment theory, in theories describing how the psyche heals, and now thanks to neuroscience, in theories about brain development. Self-mirroring must be developed for us to see our own wounded soul.

The second story, the myth of *Narcissus*, takes us deeper into the needs of the wounded soul and the process of transformation. To get through the nearly impenetrable defenses and constructions that have been built to protect that soul requires a life-and-death struggle in the psyche. The false self needs to die to the true self.

But Narcissus doesn't take us far enough. Like Virgil who brings Dante to the entry of heaven, then transfers his responsibility as guide to Beatrice, here, it is Medusa who guides us home. In order to transform narcissism, we must get to the very depths of the psyche, and the myth of *Medusa* offers a path of redemption and return.

The third story, the myth of *Medusa*, helps us look directly at what we believe will kill us if seen and offers wise suggestions about how to embark on this confrontation without annihilation. And it offers a glimpse of the power that is released when the task is successfully accomplished.

Narcissism maintains its power until it can be seen—clearly. We cannot begin to engage with, not to mention transform, an evil until we can see it and name it. We must recognize narcissism's pre-occupation with self over others. We must see narcissism at work when it acts in fear to preserve and promote self-interest. We must recognize the lack of empathy for others and the absence of mercy when its own interests seem to be at stake. Narcissism is devoid of the capacity for relatedness, which is essential for human connection.

But even when seen, narcissism remains entrenched—entwined in habits, defenses, numbing, and projection. These myths and fairy tales offer insight and guidance about the origins, character, and transformation of narcissism. At the root of narcissism is the neglect of an essential human need, the longing to be seen, known, and accepted. This is a universal need, essential to the development of the human being. Unless it is met, the development of the self, the capacity for self-regulation, and the actualization of our human potential falters.

We're learning from neuroscience that healthy brain development is dependent on effective mirroring of the self. The pathways of the brain are formed in the first years of life through interactions with our first *others*, usually parents, but any consistent caregiver can play this role. A healthy brain requires interactions that are consistent, coherent, and reflective for neural pathways that are consistent, coherent, and reflective to develop.

Mirroring is much more than something that makes us feel good. It is *essential* to the development of our true self and the development of a healthy, integrated brain.

The mirrors in *Snow White* and in the myths of *Narcissus* and *Medusa* reflect a depth-exploration of narcissism and offer insights about a way out. Many fields of study are now converging on truths similar to the ones conveyed in these myths. Psychology, attachment theory, and trauma theory offer new insights into the construction of the self-concept. In neuroscience, the discovery of mirror neurons and brain plasticity offer deeper understanding of the brain and a hope for its recovery. In quantum physics and chaos theory, the emergence of a whole that is greater than the sum of its parts has been affirmed.

We can recognize narcissism in others when it blocks our needs being met. We might say, "He's selfish," when his interests interfere with ours. Although it's hard to see our own narcissism, that is always the place to begin. No one is without narcissism. Our capacity for awareness, relatedness, and empathy are the exits from our own narcissism.

The wounds that take narcissism from the instinct for survival to pathological levels stem from failures in early development. Parenting is a very difficult job. The parent must develop the capacity to tend another's needs over their own. Effective parenting is profoundly influenced by the parent's own narcissism and his or her capacity for empathy for the child and the child's experience.

A quote by the poet Rumi, "When a mirror contains no images, all forms are contained in it," offers a glimpse of where we're headed. Some stages of psychological and spiritual development can change the perception of separateness and open the capacity for nearly pure mirroring. We must discover a mirror that is devoid of images, one that is capable of "pure seeing" of what's actually there, without adding or taking anything away. The task is to become empty, for only in emptiness is pure seeing possible. This "emptiness" is full of *being*, simple awareness, and presence. Can the mind become so still that it rests in non-dual awareness?

We must let go of fear, worry, and even thought itself, and dwell in the heart. The mind cannot take us beyond narcissism; for that, the heart is required. Standing in the heart, compassion and mercy are present. Standing empty of form, we discover all forms. Only when we're without form, intention, or motive do we have the capacity to *see*. As the Little Prince taught, "It is only with the heart that one sees clearly." Dwelling in the heart-center, shame is supplanted by unconditional love, and we return to the home we've been seeking.

Let this book take you along with Snow White, Narcissus, and Medusa into the depths to discover the core of your wounded self and recover your true self that the world so desperately needs.

"...Let go of your worries
and be completely clear-hearted,
like the face of a mirror
that contains no images.

When it is empty of forms,
all forms are contained in it.
No face would be ashamed
to be so clear..."

—Rumi[9]

---

[9] Helminski, K. (Ed.). (2000). The Inner Garment of Love. In *The Rumi Collection: An Anthology of Translations of Mevlana Jalaluddin Rumi*, p. 49. Boulder, CO: Shambhala Publications.

● ● ● ●

## Chapter 1
# The Mirror

*"Our wound is not what happened to us in the past, it is that we were unable to stay connected to our deeper nature in the face of what happened to us in the past. [The problem now] is our disconnect from the truth of who we are."*

—Jennifer Welwood[10]

*"The human wound that fuels all psychological work is that the initial environment in some way failed, consistently over time, to meet needs adequately."*

—Barbara Sullivan[11]

Snow White, Narcissus, and Medusa can teach us about narcissism and how it heals. I began working

---

[10] Welwood, J. (2003). *The Sacred Mirror: Nondual Wisdom and Psychotherapy*, p. 297. St. Paul, MN: Paragon House.
[11] Sullivan, B. S. (1989). *Psychotherapy Grounded in the Feminine Principle*. Asheville, NC: Chiron Publications.

with these stories when I realized that each has a mirror as a central character.

In 2007, Giacomo Rizzolatti, Vittoria Gallese, and Leonardo Fogassi, professors of human psychology in Parma, Italy, were awarded the University of Louisville Grawemeyer Prize in Psychology for identifying prefrontal cortex cells called *mirror neurons*, whose task it is to attune us to the inner state of others. Mirroring is the ability to grasp another's experience and reflect it back accurately. It activates when we observe behavior in others. It helps explain how we empathize and communicate and why we learn by seeing as well as doing. Vittoria Galese writes, "The other's emotion is constituted, experienced, and therefore directly understood by means of an embodied simulation producing a shared body state. It is the activation of a neural mechanism shared by the observer and observed to enable direct experiential understanding."[12]

We are equipped with the ability to experience another person's movements, sensations, and emotions. Daniel Goleman calls this the *social brain*, and adds that this neural network "forms a brain-to-brain bridge that puts us on the same wavelength.... [T]his goes on in every interaction, whether we

---

[12] Gallese, V. (2007). Embodied simulation: from mirror neuron systems to interpersonal relations. *Novartis Foundation Symposium* (278: 3-12).

know it or not."[13] *Whether we know it or not!* If we haven't developed our capacity for mirroring another, which develops by receiving mirroring, mirroring may occur in the brain anyway, even though we're unaware of it.

We're wired to mirror one another. Being mirrored in the early years of life is the basis for knowing our self. Mirroring offers us secure attachments, a sense of self, and an ability for self-regulation. Mirroring continues throughout our lifetime; it is an ongoing, constant, plastic, and mutual process. Our work is to make it conscious, and we cannot do this without others. We form a shared state with another and mirror each other in each interaction. When we are able to bring consciousness, willingness, and openness to this, we can overcome narcissism. Are the brains of those lacking empathy structurally different from those whose mirror neurons reflect others? Research is currently being done in this area.

To accurately mirror another, we must forget our self and focus on attuning to the other. Then without judgment or thought, we join with the other's experience. As we develop the capacity to express the other's experience accurately, learning

---

[13] Kiesling, S. interview with Goleman, D. (2006). Wired for compassion. In *Spirituality & Health*, September/October, p. 50.

the language of purely reflecting the other, health ensues.

Think of the example of the nursing mother who is awakened during the night by the cries of her child. Perhaps it's been only a couple hours since she put the baby to bed, and now her sleep is interrupted again. Her first response might be, "Oh no, another sleep-deprived night for me." Yet, in spite of the fatigue or exasperation, she makes herself available, lovingly standing near her baby's crib, available to attend to the distress of the child with presence, comfort, gentleness, and the willingness to respond to the child's need. We enter the world as unformed, unreflected, innocent unconsciousness. For the self and a well-developed brain to emerge, accurate mirroring is necessary.

Carl Rogers, one of the founders of humanistic psychology, defined *empathy* as being at home in the private perceptual world of the other, entering into their reality. As we enter another's world, we take them in as whole. In this way, perception becomes a coherent experience, including thoughts, feelings, beliefs, sensations, attitudes, intentions, perceptions and memories.[14] We then can mirror accurately what's being said, felt, thought, and experienced, both consciously and unconsciously. Rogers said, "When I can relax and be close to the transcendental

---

[14] Rogers, C. R. (1980). *A Way of Being.* Boston: Houghton Mifflin.

core of me, ... it seems that my inner spirit has reached out and touched the inner spirit of the other. Our relationship transcends itself and becomes a part of something larger. Profound growth and healing are present."[15] Rogers said this before the discovery of mirror neurons, just giving voice to his own empathic resonance.

Daniel Siegel names what arises between two people when empathic mirroring takes place *emotional resonance*. When tuning in to one another's internal states establishes a link, each person *"feels felt"* by the other and influences the other's internal state. It's like in music when notes harmonically reinforce each other, creating resonance, as opposed to the dissonance we hear when instruments are not in attunement.

Emotional resonance is a high calling. A lot must happen before we're able to mirror one another. We need to set aside our own thoughts and experiences, which is difficult because our reactions, feelings, and opinions don't have an off-button. As we listen, we must be capable of multitasking, having a *both/and* capacity to our awareness. We need communication skills that accurately reflect and then give voice to what we've heard and felt,

---

[15] Rogers, C. (1989). A Client-Centered Person-Centered Approach to Therapy. In H. Kirschenbaum & V. L. Henderson, *The Carl Rogers Reader*, p. 137. Boston: Mariner Books.

without opinion or embellishment, which also requires clarity in listening so we're not interpreting, judging, or evaluating but simply reflecting and reporting.

For narcissism to resolve requires being accurately mirrored and it also requires us to develop the capacity to be a mirror. We do this by first learning to mirror our self; then we can develop the ability to mirror another.

During mirroring, we come to know ourselves, trust the other, and form internal constructs and processes that form a secure base for the self. Transformations within the self also occur through mirroring.

As you consider the mirror in the myths in this book, you'll begin to know yourself as a mirror, as the reflection you seek. And as your capacity for self-reflection increases, notice how your capacity for reflecting others increases as well.

"He's just selfish," is a common way of describing narcissism. Superficially it's true, but it doesn't begin to explain the intricately constructed nature of narcissism.

As the quotes at the beginning of the chapter indicate, narcissism is a deep, well-established, hidden, and thus denied wound in the psyche around which complex constructions, dynamics, and habits are built to protect the wound's vulnerability.

When we most needed our true nature to be seen and reflected, it wasn't.

Object Relations Theory recognizes mirroring as a fundamental psychological need. The reflection of the child's experience back to the child from its caregivers during the crucial time during which the child is forming a self is essential to developing a capacity for relatedness and a capability for self-regulation. The caregiver's attunement to the child's needs and experiences provides a secure base for the child to stay engaged with his or her own experience. If this is lacking and the child's experience goes unrecognized, it falls into the unconscious. Experiences that don't receive the relational response of mirroring and empathy cannot be sustained by the child who does not yet have the capacity of self-reflection. So, these un-mirrored experiences reside in the unconscious.

Here's an example. While leaving my infant son at a daycare provider, the baby began to cry just as I was turning him over to the caregiver and moving toward the door. "He's mad at you for leaving," the caregiver said. "No," I said, moving back toward him, "he's frightened." When he was comforted and engaged with some familiar things, he was able to let me depart without protest. (By the way, he did not remain long in that environment, since I no longer trusted that he would receive accurate mirroring there.)

The failure of early attachments to mirror the child accurately, with consistency and unconditional acceptance, creates narcissistic wounding. This is not an indictment of the parents, but a recognition of the lack of understanding they may have had of the emotional and psychological needs of the child and how to meet them. Recognizing emotional needs and emotional communication is fairly new to our collective mind. Not long ago, children were "to be seen and not heard." Parenting was defined by power constructs, not relating to the child's true nature. Love and care were there, but the subtle needs of emotional development were not understood by parents whose own upbringings had not addressed those needs. Recent research about emotional needs was not yet part of common knowledge.

In the generation before mine, there was a lack of emotional communication for them and by them, and the need for emotional mirroring was not recognized as essential for children. The collective unconscious holds a tremendous void of unmirrored affect and unrealized potential. When, for example, anger and frustration are not mirrored, the unconscious might hold these feelings as unexpressed rage. When a child's true attributes and potential are not mirrored, they may remain in the unconscious, unexplored and unexpressed. Even the child's natural capacity for empathy may reside in the unconscious if he didn't experience empathy in early interactions. This lack of mirroring causes wounding in the individual and a loss for the society of true feeling well-expressed, of full potential embodied, and of a developed capacity for relatedness. Thankfully, this is changing as psychology and neuroscience learn more about the developmental process.

Because the personality and behavior of the narcissist are so overbearing and wounding to others, it's difficult to appreciate that at the root of narcissism is woundedness. Rather, the word *narcissism* is commonly used as a pejorative, meaning self-centered, arrogant, and selfish. The narcissist has a high need to be admired by others, an inflated self-worth, and a need for the constant approval of others. We can see this plainly in Donald Trump and his need to tweet in the wee hours of the morning when he feels the least slight or disapproval. In July 2016 Trump told Anderson Cooper, "I get along with everybody. People love me and you know what? I've been very successful; everyone loves me." His desperate need is apparent.

Cruz and Buser point out that the narcissist has "essentially lost connection with the corrective ministries of the Self. Thus, he or she is consumed by a default program: namely, *self-inflation as compensation for the disconnect from the Self.*"[16] The narcissist lacks an actual connection to the true self

---

[16] Buser, S. & Cruz, L. (Eds.). (2017). *A Clear and Present Danger,* p. 8.

and therefore cannot accurately perceive or experience the self, but is instead captured by distortions that serve as a defense against the void that exists as the center of his being.

Let us look at the defining characteristics of narcissism, and then move to the story of Snow White to see these characteristics at work. They include a lack of empathy and the presence of envy. Because there is a lack of a felt sense of one's worth, the other person is idealized and valued. This idealization is then envied and eventually hated. We see this in Donald Trump's oversimplification of others as either a good or a bad person. The former is the idealized other who is affirming and agreeing with the narcissist. The latter is the other who is not validating the narcissist. In either case, the other person is not experienced as real. The narcissistic personality is designed to protect itself against rage and envy, thus the constant need to affirm one's superiority and maintain control. Relatedness is defended against out of a terror of loss of power.

The weak ego cannot tolerate criticism. There is a deep fear of one's own unconscious and one's own affect, and this is often split off, inaccessible, and projected onto others. The narcissistic defense avoids feeling the unconscious affect, resulting in disconnection from one's true self. Since the affect has been insufficiently mirrored, the narcissist has no capacity for self-mirroring and lacks practice at tolerating and engaging with feeling. There is no internal structure for reflective inner mirroring, without which it's impossible to notice or experience one's own affect. Affect is either dissociated, or the narcissist is flooded by and fused with it.

Fantasies of omnipotence protect the narcissistic core. The psyche constructs methods of impenetrability to maintain itself. It's a mask covering the void behind it. Like the Wizard of Oz, it's all construction and posing; behind the curtain is the undeveloped, vulnerable, little man.

The wall that protects the narcissist's core must be invincible, because failure to maintain it feels life-threatening. If the construction fails to keep the unwanted out, the self falls into a dark void, as we'll see in the myth of Narcissus. When one is unfamiliar with the void, letting defenses down feels like ceasing to exist. The narcissist experiences the unknown as nonexistent, a core emptiness, and this accounts for a high risk of suicide when a narcissist loses the persona that has been constructed as the false self.

The *Snow White* fairy tale offers insight into the underlying wounds that create the narcissistic core, and identifies some essential elements needed for the wound to begin to heal. *Narcissus* offers insight into the threshold of self-discovery, the turning point toward redeeming the true self. *Medusa* provides insight about the depths that need to be explored in an encounter with the self for transformation to take place. As we begin to understand the need for the mirror and how it operates, we begin to track the course of the psyche through the wounded self into healing.

• • • •

## Chapter 2
# The Tale of Snow White

Let us start at the beginning. Once upon a time...

This fairy tale begins with a lovely, young queen hoping for the birth of a child, who would be Snow White. The pure-as-driven-snow center of the human being is what Jung would call an *archetype*, in this case, the innocent, nondual core of being that is at the center of the self. One day, while doing needlepoint and daydreaming of a daughter who would bring this innocence into the world, the queen pricks her finger and a drop of bright, red blood falls upon the snow outside her window.

Here is the forewarning: The pure core is always wounded.

The queen gives birth, but dies doing so. So many myths and fairy tales begin with, "The mother is dead." This accounts, in part, for the wounding. Without the attentive and protective love and attachment of a mother, the pure being at the core will be hurt, lost, and ultimately abandoned. This wounding is a formative experience in the development of the self.

A child requires attentive, empathic, compassionate relatedness and reflection if he or she is to develop a healthy coherent sense of self, develop a healthy brain, and have the capacity for relating.[17] In the absence of this, narcissistic wounding occurs. The self goes unseen, misunderstood, or abandoned and is unable to connect to itself. This creates a deep yearning within and an ongoing, desperate effort to protect oneself from further harm.

After the mother's death, the king remarries a beautiful woman, who is prideful and cruel. She has studied the black arts, owns a magic mirror, and every day asks, "Mirror, mirror on the wall, who's the fairest of them all?" Snow White lacks a mother for assurance and instead there is a flat, cold mirror which must be asked over and over again for assurance of one's beauty. The wicked stepmother personifies the narcissistic core in action. Though beautiful, she cannot hold this experience of herself and seeks constant reinforcement of her beauty from the mirror. Every other potential beauty is a threat. She's desperately driven to maintain her power,

---

[17] Siegel, D. (2013). *Parenting From the Inside Out: How a Deeper Self-Understanding Can Help You Raise Children Who Thrive.* New York: TarcherPerigee.

because she has no internalized sense of her own value.

The queen's mirror can only speak the truth. Each time she asks her mirror this question, the mirror gives the same answer, "You, O Queen, are the fairest of all." This pleases her greatly. But then one morning when she asks, the mirror says, "You, my queen are fair, it is true, but Snow White is even fairer." The queen flies into a jealous rage and orders her huntsman to take Snow White into the woods and kill her. This is a perfectly clear depiction of the drive of the narcissistic ego to preserve its own power, even at the cost of annihilating the true self, which is perceived as a threat, because it's unknown and therefore not valued. The narcissist has never had the mirroring to know its self.

Kabir Helminski defines this essential self as "the realization of a presence that is our deeper nature and includes attention, will, and self-transcendence."[18] The narcissist having no perception, conception, or connection to this essential self identifies with the ego and its defenses rather than the true self.

In *Snow White*, the true self is pure and innocent but also naïve and vulnerable. She is without a protector, as her mother is dead and her

---

[18] Helminski, K. E. (1992). *Living Presence: A Sufi Way to Mindfulness & the Essential Self*. New York: Tarcher Putnam.

father avoids her because she is so like her mother that it stirs his grief. The stepmother is too filled with envy and competitiveness to provide guidance or protection. So, the huntsman takes Snow White into the forest, but he is unable to kill her. Instead he lets her go, and all alone in the great forest, Snow White begins to run. She is literally lost in the woods.

Running over sharp stones, through thorny bushes, as evening is about to fall, she sees a little house and goes inside to rest. Everything in the house is tidy and in miniature. She falls asleep, and in the morning discovers that it's the house of seven dwarfs who mine gold in the mountains. The dwarfs offer to house her in exchange for cooking and housecleaning, and she wholeheartedly agrees.

She now has the support of the dwarfs, who are dedicated to loving and protecting her. Notice the hope offered here. Even when the self is lost, there are undeveloped but loyal parts of the psyche—seven is a beneficial and protective sacred number[19]—trying to help the self survive.

The magic mirror tells the stepmother that Snow White is still alive and still the fairest of them all. So, the wicked stepmother finds Snow White and

---

[19] Medium Maria. What is the meaning of the number 7? https://www.linkedin.com/pulse/what-meaning-number-7-medium-maria/ on 2019-03-24

attempts to smother, poison, and choke her, and finally succeeds. Another ray of hope: Snow White is asleep but not dead.

Life persists at the core self, even when it's been smothered, poisoned, and choked. It sleeps in silence until it can be awakened. It's dormant but not dead, resting in the unconscious.

The extent of narcissistic wounding falls on a continuum from mild to severe. No one is unscathed, because all parents are less than perfect and because circumstances inevitably contribute to failures in mirroring. The prognosis for recovery depends on the depth of the wounding and the accessibility of channels to recover the sleeping beauty within.

The antidote for narcissism is not an unwounded psyche. To be human is to suffer imperfections in mirroring and relatedness. Wounding is needed to draw the psyche toward and through its pain so that something new can come forth. This wound is an archetypal necessity: It takes the self more deeply into the process of discovery so it can recover its wholeness. Wounding cannot be avoided.

No matter how dedicated and loving our parents may have been, there were necessarily imperfections in mirroring. The parent's own unconscious wounds impede clear mirroring, which might have been amplified by temperamental differences between parent and child so the parent didn't accurately perceive the child's needs. It might also have been because of circumstances that couldn't be avoided, such as poverty, illness, or the death of parents by trauma or war. It might have been caused by ignorance of the child's needs and development.

To be human is to be wounded, and to understand our wounds and seek healing is the way to come to the wholeness of being human. This is the hero's journey. It propels us into the spiritual dimension of finding our limits and yielding to the transformational process the archetype of wholeness is pressing towards. Jung says that the psyche is always striving toward wholeness, that there is an archetype of wholeness at the center of the self and the psyche seeks this. *Libido*, life energy, is animated by the archetype of wholeness and provides the energy for becoming one's self and fulfilling our potential, realizing our true self.

Snow White is asleep, dormant, in a coma. Amid this tragedy, a prince arrives. This heroic figure, in Jungian terms, is a representation of the animus, the inner masculine in a woman that forms a bridge between the unconscious and conscious aspects of her psyche. (In men, the anima or feminine soul, serves the same purpose.) The positive animus is in love with the true self and dedicated to being a reflective presence in service to the soul. The prince is the one who might be able to wake the sleeping beauty within. In him, there is a protector who can see her, know her, and act on her behalf. How desperately the world needs a prince like this now, heroic energy that is a potential in each of us and is called forth in times of crisis and loss.

We might notice this prince energizing hundreds of thousands of women to march in order to be seen and heard accurately. This prince provides the energy and commitment to get up early, drive or take a train, stand in crowds, wait patiently for the space to make one's self a part of the authentic expression of dissent. The prince offers voice and action on behalf of the wounded self. He can help the wounded self be seen and heard.

The prince is captivated by Snow White's beauty and gazes upon her, enraptured. Here is a man who values the beauty of the feminine and sees her soul. This moves him to dedication. Nothing is more important than serving and protecting the soul. Unlike the narcissist, who would view the princess as an object to own, the prince wants only to care for, nurture, and bring her back to life.

Narcissism is unable to dedicate itself to inner values or to another. It's too busy sustaining the ego-inflated persona. There is a constant demand to affirm one's own value. Dedication to something greater than one self just isn't possible. There's no real sense of another. Narcissism is incapable of experiencing otherness, because others are experienced as objects. Internally, it's the same: The narcissist cannot experience anything other than the ego, because the demands of ego's defenses prevent connection with the true self.

Without the inner guidance of the self, analyst Nathan Schwartz-Salant tells us, "We have no individual compass and little hold on identity. One is drawn to be part of a collective mind, uncritically attaching to collective values of power, fame, and money, those seductive and false indicators of self-esteem. A bloated ego then takes the place of the self."[20]

The prince, on the other hand, is connected and senses the beauty—outer and inner—of this feminine soul and feels a commitment to providing for and protecting her. The dwarfs concede and allow the prince to take Snow White with him, and in the effort to move her, she is awakened from her deep sleep.

In a classic fairy tale ending, the prince and Snow White are wed. Nothing could be more important. We must see beyond the romantic notion of this union and perceive the inner union between the purity of the soul and the animus. This wedding is a transformation of the ego's power to the power

---

[20] Schwartz-Salant, N. (2017) Healthy presidential narcissism: is that possible? In S. Buser & L. Cruz (Eds.). *A Clear and Present Danger*, p. 19.

of the true self. The prince has penetrated the constructs of the ego and made a bridge of connection to the true self.

In our collective consciousness, we've projected the need for a prince onto romantic love, seeking an outer figure to satisfy our longing for self-mirroring. Even a cursory look at statistics on committed relationships show that projecting this inner need is, by and large, not working.

Only by turning inward and mobilizing our capacity for self-mirroring can the animus or anima emerge as a heroic figure that offers reflection and action for the true self to express itself in the world.

The ego can only pursue itself. It's fragile, a human construct that seeks only to protect its own needs. The Self, represented by Snow White, is an expression of the intrinsic essence and potential of the human being. The capacities for love, joy, compassion, and creativity dwell in the Self, and we are bereft until our connection to this creative center is restored.

Schwartz-Salant describes this Self as a subtle, inner presence, a guide, an organizing and orienting principle. "But the aliveness, form and presence of this mysterious orienting center of being can be greatly impeded. Abandonment or betrayal, by a person or institution, can cause the self to fragment and lose vitality, its positive features gone from awareness."[21]

The Snow White essence of the self languishes in sleep until the prince arrives. This prince is essential to our evolution and the evolution of the world. It can move us from the drive of ego to the achievement of soul. The prince represents the inner-mirroring presence that actually sees Snow White and her inner beauty and can reflect what he sees in his love for and service to her. We see in the prince the means to repair what external mirrors failed to do. He sees all of who she is and can begin a process of self-reflection that promotes the embodiment of her true self.

It's difficult for us to call forth our prince. The ego's pursuit of status and success, as defined by culture, make the prince's emergence unlikely. Connecting with our own purity, innocence, beauty, and vulnerability and wanting to protect all of that is not going to make us famous or wealthy.

Yet the stories we tell ourselves are filled with princely characters. Princes fill novels and movies. We long for them, yet fear mobilizing our own inner prince. We doubt we can succeed by the measure of the world in the presence of such a prince.

How can we mobilize the prince in our psyche? Pain, distress, and crises call him forth.

---

[21] Buser, S. & Cruz, L. (2017). *A Clear and Present Danger*, p. 18.

When the self is no longer able to tolerate the self-betrayal that continues to take place while the ego is in control, the prince might step forward. This can occur when we're locked in a mind-numbing job and can't stand another meaningless day, or perhaps an empty marriage fails again and again to honor loving intimacy, calling forth an action principle to do something different. Or it may be an act of betrayal so significant it mobilizes the prince to action out of long-buried loyalty to the self.

In the marriage of Snow White (anima, the soul) to the prince (animus, heroic action), the wicked stepmother (mind-numbing disconnect, cruel psychopathy, and dualistic fear) is slain. The emergence of the powerful prince in service to the soul redeems the world and defeats narcissism. The wicked stepmother—narcissism—remains in control until the snow-white beauty of the soul is recognized. When it's truly seen and felt, it calls forth a mirror, a protector, in the princely animus who sees, loves, and serves the soul. This is the repair of the allegiance to the self that is betrayed when the self goes unmirrored and the ego is allowed to reign.

We can see in the Christ story a profound example of the dedication of a prince to a snow-white soul. Christ can be seen as the animus linking the human soul to God. Like an internal animus, Christ is a bridge that connects humanity and divinity whose purpose is the redemption of the soul and the establishment of relatedness between the soul and its creator. At the time of Christ's birth, the soul had lost its identity as a child of the divine. Christ reflects the true human being, both human *and* divine. He offers himself, giving his own life to preserve the pure white soul that reflects the creator.

In the *Snow White* fairy tale, we recognize how endangered the pure soul is in the world. This story depicts the narcissistic drive, portrayed by the stepmother who is so absorbed pursuing her own worth that she would slay the pure soul to stay on top. The longed-for prince needs to emerge to protect the soul and defeat the narcissistic drive.

Now we know the characters, the power struggle we're engaged in, and what is required to gain a successful resolution. Next, we need to understand how it's done, and for that, we turn to the myth of *Narcissus*.

● ● ● ●

## Chapter 3

# Witnessing

*...“Save us from what our own hands might do;*
*lift the veil, but do not tear it.*
*Save us from the ego; its knife has reached our*
*bones.*
*Who but you will break these chains?*
*Let us turn ourselves to You*
*Who are nearer to us than ourselves.*
*Even this prayer is Your gift to us.*
*How else has a rose garden grown from these*
*ashes?...”*

—Rumi[22]

How do I know who I am? Of what is our I-ness composed? This question has been studied for eons.

[22] Helminski, K. (Ed.). (2008). Your mysterious giving. In *The Pocket Rumi*, p. 146. Boulder, CO: Shambhala.

As we saw in the fairy tale *Snow White*, there is a battle between the wounded ego and the true self to claim I-ness. Each human being is possessed by the question *Who am I?* Rumi says the ego has claimed us to the bone. Can the self emerge from the ashes to re-claim us?

Richard Miller, a psychologist and the developer of Integrative Restorative Yoga Nidra (iRest® Yoga Nidra), suggests that there are two components of I-ness. There is our immanent experience in thoughts, feelings, and sensations. And there's transcendent experience, which is the observing, or witnessing, of experience.

Kabir Helminski calls this mindfulness, our ability to observe our experience rather than simply experience it, an inherent *awareness*, not a construction. He calls this *purified subjectivity*, "Freed of our habitual thoughts, expectations, opinions, constructions, and fears."

In yoga philosophy, this pure subjectivity is called *vijnyanamaya kosha*, the inner witness. This is pure awareness that welcomes what is, just as it is. We can understand this as the essential self, which must be recovered to defeat the ego and overcome narcissism.

Spiritual teachers speak of this awareness as something we come to by awakening. Though it is always with us, we may not be conscious of it, because we have become so fused with our experience that we can't hold a standpoint for observing experience. When this capacity for mindful observing is not present, it's due to the lack of reflective capacity in the psyche.

The experience of being mirrored or reflected accurately is necessary for developing the capacity of self-reflection. If it's lacking, instead of this reflective capacity with an energized presence at its center, there's a void which feels empty. *Witnessing consciousness* remains unconscious. This helps us understand why the narcissist is so out of touch with his impact on others. The experiential is neither felt, observed, nor witnessed.

Schwartz-Salant describes two phases of recovery for healing narcissism. In the first phase, there is a separation from the fusion and identification with the persona. Until this can be achieved, we know ourselves only as the ego/persona. There's no connection with the contents of self-experience, only the persona's posturing which focuses on how we appear in the world.

To navigate this phase of separation from fusion with the persona, an authentic relationship with our self is needed. This can occur in a relationship with a therapist during which the contents of our experiential self that have been unconscious begin to be mirrored in a way that can be felt and integrated. In the persona, there is no direct experience of the felt contents of our life and no voice for this.

During this phase of separating from the persona, a capacity for reflecting our actual experience is being developed, and empathy for our self is being established. For example, our persona's standpoint might have been to live up to and achieve all that our father expected in order to win his approval. During this stage of separation and reflection, we begin to notice and experience how that's been for us, what we think and feel about it, what is really true for us about these expectations and achievements?

The power of denial, repression, and dissociation can be airtight so that the actual feeling of our own experience is outside of consciousness. When our felt experience has been unconscious, how can we access it? This is the work of self-discovery.

There are still what poker players call *tells*. The soul is making itself known even when there are no eyes to see it. Bessell van der Kolk says it well in the title of his book on trauma, *The Body Keeps the Score*. Locked into our anatomy, the felt experience may appear as tension, pain, gastrointestinal distress, or other physical symptoms. Dreams and nightmares may portray the drama of the disowned self. Intense affect, out of proportion to the situations, may hint at a deeper well of affect not yet expressed. Anxiety disorder may be the rattling lid of the pot as its hidden contents threaten to boil over. Or depression may bury what cannot be tolerated. Addiction also serves to numb experience and thus keep it hidden from us.

It's only by bringing attention and awareness to these tells, these symptoms, that we can begin to encounter the heretofore unconscious affect. When insight or awareness is achieved, there is an awakening —an epiphany—and a blossoming relationship with one's self. "The day came when the risk to remain tight in a bud was more painful that the risk it took to blossom," a statement attributed to Anaïs Nin, perfectly describes the process.

The ability to be aware of our own feelings and experiences is an essential part of being human and a necessity for forming relationships with others. Only in this ability to be present to the experiential self do we find our capacity to be present to another.

If creating space from the ego/persona can be achieved, the beginning of integration of one's own unconscious experience can begin, and the movement toward the second phase of development becomes possible.

A mystery opens up when one begins to see and feel one's self. The *possibility* of falling in love with our self emerges, but there is still the need to encounter all the disparate and conflicting aspects of the self, no easy task to accomplish. Rather than remaining fused with the constructed persona that has no capacity for seeing itself or exploring its own truth, the observing ego needs to descend into its own depths.

Terror dwells at the threshold of descent, and for this reason many stop there. How can I face the dark void of the unknown? In that consuming darkness, will "I" be destroyed? How can I let go of the posturing of the persona that seems to offer me safety, even if it is, upon examination, vacant and ungrounded? Who would I be, what would I have, who will be there for me if I'm no longer this familiar, comfortable persona? As Schwartz-Salant says, it's at this point that unknown energies "shake the very core of the conscious personality."

Many "breakdowns," going crazy, falling apart episodes are an entry to this threshold without the preparation, understanding, or resources to tolerate the persona's undoing in the face of the real contents of the psyche.

Jung himself shares his experience of crossing this threshold in *The Red Book*, the journal he kept during his own individuation journey. He says at the outset, "The years of which I have spoken to you, when I pursued the inner images, were the most important time of my life. Everything else is derived from this. It began at that time, and the later details hardly matter anymore. My entire life consisted in elaborating what had burst forth from the unconscious and flooded me like an enigmatic stream and threatened to break me. That was the stuff and material for more than one life. Everything later was merely the outer classification, the scientific elaboration, and integration into life. But the numinous beginning, which contained everything, was then."[23]

The separation from the persona is a tender time in the process of self-development. Letting go of the safety of the constructed persona and daring to enter the murky contents of one's own experience can feel life-threatening. It also holds the potentiality and possibility of meeting one's soul. The Self begins to be experienced as a living, breathing being, part of the whole of creation instead of as a construct, a thing, a facade, a sham. This encounter with the experiential core is expressed in poetry, myth, and music as Seeking the Beloved.

Jung speaks of the archetype of Wholeness, the Soul, as an instinct seeking actualization, so we might understand that it is seeking us, perhaps more intently than we are seeking it.

Support for this process of encountering the Self is needed, because it's often messy and frightening. It's like jumping out of the small boat of the ego, which has held us (though there may be holes in the boat), into the sea to make our way to sturdy ground.

---

[23] Jung, C.G. (2009). *The Red Book*, p. vii. New York: W.W. Norton.

There is considerable anxiety and a need for guidance about how to navigate this course. Schwartz-Salant says, "The Self manifests as both a seemingly well-ordered continuous process and one which can burst upon the ego with unknown energies and shake the very core of the conscious personality."[24]

A new relationship between ego and self will be negotiated as self-recognition progresses. Jung says, "The experience of the self is always a defeat for the ego."[25] The ego loses its place as king of the hill. A transformation begins in which the ego accepts its position to serve the Self, instead of the other way around.

---

[24] Schwartz-Salant, N. (1982). *Narcissism and Character Transformation: The Psychology of Narcissistic Character Disorders*. Toronto, ON: Inner City Books.
[25] Jung, C.G. (1977). *Mysterium Coniunctionis, Collected Works, Vol. 14* (2nd ed.) p. 778. NJ: Princeton University Press.

• • • •

## Chapter 4
# The Myth of Narcissus

This encounter with the Self is the stuff of the myth of *Narcissus*. Most have heard of this character Narcissus, the young man so entranced by his own image in a reflecting pond that he falls into the depths and dies. This myth offers us insight into the encounter of the ego with the Self and the depths of transformation initiated by this encounter. But first, let's look at Narcissus's backstory.

Narcissus's mother is a nymph who was ravaged by a river god when she was sixteen. Once again, we have a mother who is not up to the task of protecting herself or her child. The masculine in the form of the river god takes what he wants and this nymph is overwhelmed. So, Narcissus is raised by an immature, dominated mother, and a power-driven father. With such roots, how could he know himself?

Narcissus goes wandering in the woods and encounters Echo, a nymph who has only the ability to repeat what she has heard. This was an enchantment ordered by a goddess who grew tired of her over-talkativeness, and she limited Echo's speech. Narcissus calls out, "Is anyone here?" and Echo replies, "Here." Narcissus says, "Let us meet," and she echoes, "Let us meet."

Echo is enchanted with the handsome young man and seeks to embrace him. To this Narcissus says, "Embrace me not. May I die before I give you power o'er me." And Echo replies, "Power o'er me."

There you have it, the self-absorbed narcissist who allows no one to touch him. And, the undeveloped feminine who is enchanted but without a voice of her own. Echo is the character of many women who are married to narcissistic men. Often, it's Echo who will come for therapy, because she's married to someone for whom she doesn't really exist, and her own narcissistic wounds keep her bound in the relationship.

Narcissus is looking for himself, not another. He comes upon a small reflecting pond and gazing into it, he sees an image and is entranced. He loves the image in the pool, and can't stop gazing at it, not to eat, drink, or depart. Death finds him still gazing deeply into the pool.

The death of Narcissus represents a step on the path of the transformation of the narcissistic ego. It can be understood as a letting go of the attachment to the ego and a falling into the depths of the

Self. Better to die as he risks falling into the exploration of his own depths than to continue never knowing himself.

This first encounter with one's Self is profound, visceral, and dramatic, a turning point in the psyche, a moment of truth. Once experienced, the Self can no longer be denied, and that has a transformative effect.

I am reminded of a woman I worked with who had invested a great deal to achieve her status as a successful attorney. She was struggling with anxiety and depression. As she began to encounter and stay with her own experience, she was one day able to say, "I hate what I'm doing." The requirements of success in her career were completely counter to her own inner interests, values, and temperament. She struggled for a long time against letting herself know and feel this truth. All the years of education and ambition and money spent made it difficult to look into the face of her actual experience. Once she encountered and accepted the truth, she found a way to leave that work behind and invest in a path that was truer to her Self.

Dan Siegel speaks of *Mindsight*, the ability of the mind to see and experience itself, as essential to human development. He says, a person "must develop the ability to devote himself thoroughly and fully to a particular perception, to take it in completely, and to sense what it causes to take place in him. And he must let the inner image that arises as this happens fuse with all the other images that are already there inside him, so that they make one whole integrated picture, which is then more like a feeling. When this happens, he must not allow himself to become so aroused by this feeling that he becomes identified with it and loses himself in it; rather he must be able to detach himself from it, yet nevertheless preserve it within him from then on.... All of us were able to do this, at least on a rudimentary level, when we were children. Many of us, however, have lost the ability.... It is possible to restore this ability."[26]

Siegel is describing the internal experience of perceiving our self and the subtle attention that's required to preserve that. We must be looking into our own inner reflecting pool to see deeply, and with a felt sense, integrate what we see.

Narcissus represents a moment at the threshold encounter with a true perception of the self, and he is taking it in completely. It causes him to feel deeply his love and attachment for this perceived self. This is a pivotal moment in self-discovery and in the healing of narcissism.

We've all had those Aha moments of self-recognition. It could be seeing ourselves with our

---

[26] Siegel, D. J. (2010). *Mindsight: The New Science of Personal Transformation* (pp. 109-110). New York: Bantam Books.

own eyes rather than through someone else's. It could be experiencing our own affect and really connecting with that. For example, when someone is describing a childhood experience and when prompted, acknowledges the sadness that was present and is able to say, "I am sad."

Narcissus presents us with the necessity and the potency of that encounter as it's experienced in the psyche. However, he is too overcome by the experience to do anything other than stare into the pool. But he doesn't realize the beauty he's captivated by is actually himself. There is no voice within him that can say, "I'm beautiful." He's looking at a reflection but not integrating it into himself. His capacity for self-reflection has not been developed. He has glimpsed the Beloved, but does not yet know it as himself. At the same time, he's so overcome by the experience he can't do anything other than stare into the pool.

In this encounter the ego is slain by the Self, the preoccupations of the ego fall away, and only the glimpse of the Self remains. Thankfully, we are no longer enthralled by the ego, but the unconscious depths of the Self remain deep below in that pool, not yet fully known and certainly not integrated.

To take the next steps we have to meet the feared Medusa. As we leave Narcissus, he has died, at one with his Self. As Dorothy Hunt describes,

"When what is awake directly touches its own experience of anything, there is a deep intimacy with what is. By directly, I mean when the thinking mind is not engaged in its usual efforts to separate, label, categorize, judge, dampen, exaggerate, deny, change, manipulate, or create stories about the experience of the moment. To experience something is not to discharge it, deny it, act it out, redirect it, represent it, judge it, analyze it, make commentary about it, or 'understand' it with the mind. It is to be one with it, to experience it fully. This direct experience is always transformative."[27]

Narcissus sees himself and the ego dies. But he still has no inner capacity for knowing himself and manifesting this into the world.

He has fallen into his own experiential world and now it has him. So far, we only know that it has overwhelmed him. We need the guidance of dark places and dark heroes to learn how to navigate this new way of being and to integrate the new experience of Self that has been revealed. To take the next steps we have to meet the feared Medusa.

---

[27] Hunt, D. (2003). Being intimate with what is. In *The Sacred Mirror: Non Dual Wisdom and Psychotherapy*, p. 164. St. Paul, MN: Paragon House.

●　●　●　●

# Chapter 5
# The Descent

*"To confront a person with his shadow is to show him his own light."*

—C.G. Jung[28]

> *"I am absent but deep in this absence*
> *There is the waiting for myself*
> *And this waiting is another form of presence*
> *The waiting for my return"*

—Vicente Huidobro[29]

---

[28] Jung, C.G. (1970). Good and evil in analytical psychology. In *Civilization in Transition: The Collected Works of C. G. Jung*, Vol. 10, 2nd ed., p. 872. NJ: Princeton University Press.

[29] Huidobro, V. (1982). Poetry is a heavenly crime. In Guss, D. M. (Ed.), p. 209. *The Selected Poetry of Vicente Huidobro*. New York: New Directions.

*"[T]he narcissism of everyday life is an experience of the soul, experiencing itself from within and through the self-representation. Self-realization is a rending of this veil."*

—A. H. Almaas[30]

*"Within each human being is a vast Creative Power, a hidden treasure, but this treasure is not something we can possess. It is sweet, but it is not something we can eat. By appropriating its qualities to ourselves, we short-circuit the system. When we claim no qualities as our own, we will have the qualities of this Creative Power."*

—Kabir Helminski[31]

Thank heaven we've been prepared by Snow White and Narcissus for the descent, because encountering Medusa is not for the faint of heart. It's a confrontation with the unconscious, dying to our lifelong identification with the known persona and transforming our allegiance to the essential Self. If only we can find the courage to approach her.

---

[30] Almaas, A.H. (2000). *The Point of Existence: Transformations of Narcissism in Self-Realization*, p. 64. Boulder, CO: Shambhala.
[31] Helminski, K. E. (2017). *Living Presence: The Sufi Path to Mindfulness and the Essential Self* (Rev. ed.), p. 172. New York: Tarcher Perigee.

In the tale of *Snow White*, we saw the depth and unsightliness of our own wound and the purity of the essential Self. Snow White was much too naïve to approach Medusa on her own, but with the prince as a protector she might be able to.

Overwhelmed by the depths of the Self, Narcissus dared enter into that threshold encounter, sacrificing himself in the process.

Medusa, in all her glory, can take us into the depths and darkness of the journey of transformation that neither Snow White nor Narcissus could on their own. Facing her, we'll unleash powers that reveal narcissism for what it is, the shadow of self-realization.

This is a journey of recovery from pathological narcissism, "when the self-representation is absent, weak, fragmented, disintegrated, or unrealistic, or when it is particularly vulnerable to such disturbances."[32] As smooth and self-possessed as the narcissist may seem, his or her internal self-representation is weak, absent, or lost.

Recovery will lead to a healthy narcissism, described by Almaas as "when [an individual] has developed a stable self-concept that is realistic, resistant to dissolution or disintegration, with inner harmony and positive self-regard."[33] We're seeking

---

[32] Almaas, A. H. (2000). *Point of Existence*, p. 56.
[33] ibid.

to experience a felt sense of a stable self that is both integrated and positive.

We talked about Schwartz-Salant's two levels of healing in transforming narcissism. In the first, there's a shift from ego/persona-dominated being to a relationship in which the ego operates in service to the Self. This shift is necessary to deconstruct the narcissistic stance.

When the ego is the seat of the self, its primary purpose is to serve what it believes are its own interests. The true Self, and the many elements of that Self, remain unconscious. When the ego encounters the Self, it surrenders to the self's power and becomes its servant. This rearrangement is necessary for values and purposes other than "power-over" to be expressed. In the myth of Narcissus, we see the ego falling in love with the depths of the self but failing to redefine or integrate this experience and update the definition of self.

In the second level of transformation, there is a recognition of and an encounter with the true self. Experiencing one's self is now possible, and a more authentic relationship with the self is developed. We move from defending against the experiential self into its depths. Now aware of the self, we begin to be guided, directed, and moved by the self. There is now a relationship between the ego and the self and the ability for self-expression in the world.

The midlife crisis can be such an encounter with the self. At this stage of development, the ego has established itself in the world and begins to feel a tension. Something doesn't fit; something important hasn't been achieved; or there is an emptiness and we long for something more. If we can hold the tension and gaze into the depths of the self, breaking through the ego's posturing might be achieved and something new can emerge.

Jung's work helps us understand that there is an ongoing developmental process throughout our lives. We begin as infants immersed in the unconscious, undifferentiated self. At that stage there is only pure being. There are no thoughts, concepts, or contrivances other than being the essence of who we are. As the child interacts with caregivers, the ego, a *representation* of the self, begins to develop. Now, "Being" begins to conceive of itself, to conceptualize itself, and to internalize messages, expectations, and projections received.

During the process of development, parts of the self remain unmirrored. If there are no eyes to see certain aspects of the self, those parts languish in the unconscious and the ego/persona assumes the position of the self's center. This is always a representation of the self, not the fullness of the self.[34]

---

[34] Almaas, A.H. (2000). *Point of Existence.*

When we have a direct encounter with the self, a reorganization within the psyche takes place. This was Narcissus's experience gazing at the reflection of the self he hadn't seen before. This creates a disruption in self-representation and a chance to cross the threshold into the possibility of expressing the true self.

The process of development takes us from pure being to the wounded self of representation and ego. To function in the world, egoic self-representations posture as the self. At some point, there is an encounter with the self, and if resources are present for facing this and integrating the experience, a realignment with the Self can begin.

When I refer to "Self" with a capital "S," I'm speaking of all of the potential of the true Self. This can't be captured or contained in one human self. It is the whole that is greater than the sum of its parts. When speaking of Self, we are referring to an unconstructed field of awareness, a formless capacity we can relate to but not fully integrate. Jung called the Self an archetype, a preexisting pattern in the unconscious that seeks expression in form through our instinctive nature. It is in our relationship to the Self that our own potentials lie. Almaas describes the ego carrying a representation of the self and says it's always partial. Self-representations are our narrative, our accumulated partial selves, but they're not the Self.

Our self-representations determine the experience of the self. Take for example *good girl*. A "good girl" simply doesn't experience anger; anger doesn't exist in the representation of good girl. For her, anger remains a neglected shadow until she is ready to encounter the actual contents of the self and experience the rage and terror that are stored there.

The psyche remains locked in narcissistic patterns and defenses until the core self can be seen and experienced, and not through self-representations. Almaas says, "The most deeply impoverishing alienation in ego experience is alienation from the essential core of the self."[35] The shell of self-representation masquerades as the central identity, and it feels like a pretense because the actual experience of the Self is absent. This helps us understand the desperation, neediness, and unrelenting narcissistic behavior seeking to fill the void at the center of this alienation from the Self.

How do we access the contents of the self while constructed defenses impede us? Mirroring is necessary. When my daughter was four, she offered a perfect glimpse into this necessary process. We were on our way to the first day of a new preschool. Glancing over at her, I saw that she was pale and unusually quiet. "Are you scared about your first day at school, Sweetie," I asked. "No," she said. I paused,

---

[35] Almaas, A. H. (2000). *Point of Existence*, p. 125.

wondering and then asked, "How would you know if you were scared?" She replied, "I don't know."

She did not yet have the self-mirroring construct to reflect her experience to her, nor the language to describe that experience. Had it been left at that, the experience of the self would have remained invisible. This time, though, I said, "Sometimes when we're scared, it feels like butterflies are flying around in our tummy." "Oh, I have that," she said.

The four-year-old had a lovely little emerging ego and would have rallied to handle the first day without acknowledging her actual experience. She could have lived with the untruth, "I'm not scared." A persona/shell that acts as if it's not afraid while being out of touch with feeling afraid could be formed and carry on. Or, she might have been overcome by fear in that still fragile four-year-old ego and then seen herself going forward as *afraid*. In this case, neither happened, because the four-year-old said it right. "I *have* that." Not "I *am* that." The feeling of butterflies was present and she could notice that. The self was present and in relationship to its own experience. This is the gift of mirroring. It frees the self to its essential nature, which is simply *being*, consciousness, presence, awareness, and reflecting what's actually occurring in the moment. Until the psyche can mirror itself, it cannot realize itself.

In *The New Earth*, Eckhart Tolle describes a moment of self-recognition when he was 25. He saw a woman, who was obviously insane, on the bus talking to herself.

"I was still thinking about her when I was in the men's room prior to entering the school library. As I was washing my hands, I thought: 'I hope I don't end up like her.' The man next to me looked briefly in my direction, and I suddenly was shocked when I realized that I hadn't just thought those words, but mumbled them aloud. 'Oh, my God. I'm already like her,' I thought. Wasn't my mind as incessantly active as hers? There were only minor differences between us.... For a moment, I was able to stand back from my own mind and see it from a deeper perspective as it were. There was a brief shift from thinking to awareness. I was still in the men's room, but alone now, looking at my face in the mirror. At that moment of detachment from my mind I laughed out loud. It may have sounded insane, but it was the laughter of sanity, the laughter of the big-bellied-Buddha. 'Life isn't as serious as my mind makes it out to be.' That's what the laughter seemed to be saying. But it was only a glimpse, very quickly forgotten. I would spend the next three years in anxiety and depression, completely identified with my mind. I had to get close to suicide before awareness returned, and then it was much more than a glimpse. I became free of compulsive thinking and of the false, mind-made I."[36]

We've wandered into some pretty heady stuff. Self, self-representations of the self, the capacity for self-mirroring, identification with the mind. Why is all of this really important?? Is self- realization really navel-gazing, our ego in sheep's clothing? What's being sought here? And, why?

If we go back to Jung's theory that there's an archetype of wholeness at the center of the self that is always seeking its own wholeness, then we realize that the Self is never content until wholeness is experienced. What I've seen in many years as a psychotherapist is that the self persists in developing emotional, mental, spiritual, or physical symptoms, expressing its brokenness in search of wholeness. There is no contentment without wholeness. We can find another lover, a bigger house, a new job, or even a new spiritual practice, but without experiencing wholeness, we're always in pursuit of something to fill the void.

The collective unconscious, the part of consciousness common to all mankind, is *also* in search of wholeness. Check out the self-help books that line bookstore shelves. Listen to the latest song that says, "You are my everything." Look at statistics on

---

[36] Tolle, E. (2008). *A New Earth: Awakening to Your Life's Purpose*, p. 33. New York: Penguin.

addiction and anxiety disorders. Read the many articles and blogs explaining spiritual awakening. Discovering wholeness has become a worldwide preoccupation.

Our social structures labor under the weight of power abuses, old paradigms, and an increasing gap between haves and have-nots. Social transformation, just like personal transformation, requires the healing of narcissism and the discovery of the creative power at the heart of the human being that overrides further pursuit of the ego's demands. Almaas speaks of the alienation from the core self, acknowledging how the psyche is bereft if it doesn't experience the true Self. Psyche longs for connection with its own soul. It's the alienated psyche that is the source of our social ills, prejudices, addictions, consumerism, family disruptions, and divorces.

The landmark event in the development of the psyche and the recovery of the true self is self-mirroring. This capacity is based on the child's experience of being mirrored by her or his parents. It's the capacity of the brain/self to notice and reflect its own experience. In brain research, this is recognized as *observing awareness*. In psychology, it is named the *observing ego* and recognized as a necessary capacity for development. And in spirituality, this is called *mindfulness*, moments when we have our experience and are also watching our experience. Jung called it the *transcendent function*.

"Jung refers to the transcendent function as the mediating force between the oppositions in the psyche. The transcendent function arises out of intense and concentrated conflicts within the individual. Like the koan of the Zen master, extreme and painful paradoxes can lead us to a place where we must transcend the ego so that our perception of reality is no longer split into two opposing forces."[37] For example, caught in a decision about whether to stay or leave, a third, a transcendent solution may emerge: We may stay but act differently.

The transcendent function is forged in a struggle that takes place within the psyche of an individual. Narcissistic pain can trigger such a struggle. Through the confrontation between and resolution of opposing points in an individual, the transcendent function is activated and one moves from an *either/or* tension to a *both/and* resolution.

The tension between ego and self is another example. The ego wants safety, power, and success, while the self wants to know its own truth, risk self-expression, and be directed by its own deeper values. Mobilizing the transcendent function can resolve this tension. By holding the tension between ego and self, a new consciousness can emerge that accommodates whatever arises from the unconscious.

---

[37] Perluss, B. (2006). Touching earth finding spirit: A passage into the symbolic landscape. In *Spring Journal, Fall*, p. 76.

When the capacity for self-mirroring is in place—think of Narcissus's sacrifice—the true self can now be felt. One is no longer *thinking* about one's self, but is in the experiential brain, in touch with the experiential self. This is a new state of being. Stanley Kunitz, who twice served as U.S. poet laureate, describes this contact with the unconscious mind:

"One of the great delights in poetry is that when you're really functioning, you're tapping into the unconscious in a way that is distinct from the ordinary, the customary, use of the mind in daily life. You're somehow cracking the shell separating you from the unknown. There's no formula for accessing the unconscious. The more you enter the unconscious life, the more you believe in its existence and know it walks with you, the more available it becomes and doors open faster and longer. It learns you are a friendly host. It manifests itself instead of hiding from your tyrannical presence, intruding on your daily routines, accommodations, domestications. The unconscious is very much akin to what, in other frameworks, I call *wilderness* in that its beasts are not within our control. It resists the forms, the limits, the restraints that civilization itself imposes. I've always felt, even as a child, that there was the decorum of the social structure, the family structure, and so forth, and then there was the wild permissiveness of the inner life. I learned I could go anywhere in my inner life."[38]

As infants we're identified with the unconscious. Over time, we become aware of our surroundings and begin to interact and form attachments, consciousness emerges, and our separation from the unconscious begins. Attachment theory offers insight about how attachments assist in the development of the brain. Our sense of ourselves begins in dyadic interactions—caretaker-child relating. Prior to this, we're in a unitive state in which we are as we are and there is no sense of separation. As we begin to interact with an *other*, we begin the dyadic development essential to brain and psyche development and to our own capacity for self-mirroring. It is self-mirroring that can return us to a unitive state of self-realization.

According to Almaas, "The 'fall' into narcissism happens as the self forms concepts and structures of concepts and then identifies with them at the cost of awareness of Being."[39] Self- mirroring and the transcendent function return us to our capacity for pure being, and thereby deconstruct the narcissistic structures. In this movement in the psyche, the self moves from being a construct or

[38] Kunitz, S. (2007). *The Wild Braid: A Poet Reflects on a Century in the Garden*, p. 87. New York: W.W. Norton.
[39] Almaas, A. H. (2000). *Point of Existence*, p. 15.

representation to an *ontological presence*, "a living organism that constitutes a field of perception and action,"… "a field of awareness capable of what we call experience."[40]

The self is a dynamic and fairly simple center. Jung understood it as the organizing principle at the center of the human being. Unlike many contemporary teachers and unlike eastern religions who describe *ego* pejoratively as the clinging aspects of self, Jung called this organizing principle the *ego*, Latin for I. Residing here are essential qualities like love, compassion, truth, and joy. To encounter the self, we don't actually have to dig deeply into the depths. What is necessary is the dissolution of the structures and representations that impede or distort the true self-experience. For example, the good girl persona which requires pleasing, accommodating, and being nice, and disallows anger. It's in the dissolution of the fusing with the persona that one's selfishness and anger can be experienced.

Attachment theorists have observed the presence of the self in infants. Margaret Mahler reports, "Observing infants in our set-up, we come to recognize at some point during the differentiation sub phase a certain new look of alertness, persistence, and goal-directedness. We have taken this look to be a behavioral manifestation of 'hatching'

---

[40] ibid.

and have loosely said that an infant with this look 'has hatched.'"[41]

The essential identity, "the capacity of the self to recognize itself without reference to any experience of past, or any self-image, or even any memory" is present.[42] There is no thought, censoring, or representation, but simply *experiencing* in the moment. This experiencing self is operating in the brain/body but is not a result of thinking. Science writer Diane Ackerman says, "The real wonder of the brain may be the ease with which it crafts a fluent, persuasive, stable sense of self."[43]

What has become clear from brain research is that every experience we human beings have is expressed in neurobiology. Our experiences influence how coherent, regulated, and organized the brain is. And there is an ongoing capacity for the brain to change and develop over our lifespan.

We are dependent on the capacities of the brain for the development of our sense of self, and at the same time, the brain can be the greatest roadblock in our development of a sense of self. Depending on our experiences and how they are stored in the brain, faulty and fraudulent definitions and concepts may form. In the good girl example,

---

[41] Quoted in Almaas, A.H. (2000). *Point of Existence*, p. 135.
[42] ibid, p. 138.
[43] Ackerman, D. (2005). *An Alchemy of Mind: The Marvel and Mystery of the Brain*, p. 126. New York: Scribner's.

all aspects of the self that don't meet this formulation are banished and remain unknown without penetrating the arduous defenses we maintain.

Fortunately, the brain/mind also has the capacity to transform itself. Because the brain/mind is continually forming through experience, it is also continually changing. How the mind, psyche, and self change and transform is a topic of much study and theory. Looking at several of these theories, we'll see some common features.

Mythologist Joseph Campbell has described the path of self-development and transformation as the "hero's journey." Noted Jungian analyst Donald Sandner studied primitive healing practices that included rituals, symbols, transformative rebirth experiences, and the return to the ordinary world. In mythology, we encounter the exploration of transformation in such stories as *Innana* and *Persephone and Demeter*. In object relations theory, the process of transference is seen as a transformative path for healing. Jung studied alchemy as a path of personal transformation. Each of these has the following characteristics in common, and in understanding these, we gain insight into what is required for transformation.

In each path of transformation, a *containing space* is needed. In alchemy, it's a glass flask in which compounds are mixed, while in object relations it's the therapeutic relationship.

A deep regression or *descent* is required. Campbell writes of the hero's fall as that necessary descent and says that we possess a lack of true humanity until this descent occurs. During it, one's armor is shed and a *wounded center* is revealed. Almaas describes this as the falling away of constructs and representations to the experience of what's actually present. Then, there's a *direct experience of the self* and a surrender to this, as we saw with Narcissus.

A transformative encounter with the unconscious can occur in many ways: A dream is one. During a time, I was struggling with trying to be all I felt was expected of me while, at the same time, surrendering to being my self, I had a recurring dream. I am in Baltimore's old Memorial Stadium, the only person there. I'm admiring the lovely, green baseball field and the spaciousness of the empty arena. Then I notice there's water on the field, and the water begins to rise, slowly at first. I climb up the steps in the stands and there's more and more water. Eventually I'm tightly pressed in the upmost corner of the stadium and at this point, recurring in the dream for months, I wake up with my heart pounding.

Then one night, again I'm in the upper corner of the stadium with my heart pounding, and in the dream the thought arises, "I can swim." I enter the water and float on my back, and when I wake up this time, I'm suffused with peace, contentment, and bliss.

The terror of the ego surrendered to the self and discovered what it was always looking for but never finding. All transformative paths require a *surrender*. The surrender is followed by a *rebirth* and a return to life.

In healing narcissism, our individual brain/mind/body is the crucible for transformation. A spark of consciousness can become the alchemical catalyst, and something new is created. This is a path that requires vulnerability, and as we have discussed, the narcissistic character resists this. In order to venture into the descent and allow the vulnerability required for transformation, support and resources are needed.

The story of Medusa describes the process of individuation in which the whole becomes greater than the sum of its parts. It also offers precautions and resources, so we might approach this task with protection.

• • • •

## Chapter 6
# The Myth of Medusa

King Acrisius is told by an oracle that he will be killed by his own grandson. To prevent the birth of this grandson, he imprisons his daughter Danaë and drives away all suitors. But Zeus, the supreme ruler of the gods, wants Danaë. He enters her room in a rain shower and takes her. The result of their union is Perseus.

When Acrisius discovers the child, he bundles mother and baby into a chest and casts them into the sea. Zeus sends winds to blow the chest safely to shore. The ruling king of the island on which they land takes them in and gives them shelter.

Perseus grows up to be brave and strong. The king of the island makes unwanted advances toward Danaë and plots to be rid of her son, Perseus. So, he challenges Perseus to the task of slaying Medusa, for which he will grant his mother's freedom. The king thinks this a safe bet, assuming Perseus cannot succeed, and so he anticipates making Danaë his own.

Medusa, one of three Gorgon sisters, was once beautiful, but after a rendezvous with Poseidon, god of the sea, Athena was offended and cast a spell that made Medusa so hideous that a single glance at her face would cause the onlooker to be turned to stone. Athena also turned Medusa's hair into a coiling mass of snakes.

Perseus accepts the king's challenge because of his love for his mother. He asks assistance from the gods. Zeus hears his plea and encourages Hades, Hermes, and Athena to assist him. Hades lends Perseus a helmet that renders the wearer invisible. Hermes provides him with winged sandals. And Athena gives him a shield that serves as a mirror as well as a sword.

Thus equipped, Perseus approaches Medusa, gazing not at her directly but only at her reflection in the mirror. Doing so, he's able to slice off her head and place it in his bag. As her head is being severed, blood spurts from her neck and gives birth to two sons of Poseidon, a warrior named Chrysaor and a winged horse named Pegasus.

On his way home, Perseus comes upon Andromeda chained to a rock, because Andromeda's mother's arrogance has offended the gods. Perseus uses Medusa's head to slay a sea monster and free Andromeda. They later marry and have a long life together. He gives Medusa's head to Athena, and she mounts it on her shield.

Medusa was greatly feared and couldn't be looked upon. Jung called that the *shadow*, the aspect of the unconscious where parts of the self that are feared, disallowed, and unknown reside. Medusa, and the shadow, contain great power; none dare approach them under threat of death.

Medusa was cast into her condition because she dared couple with Poseidon, god of the sea, and in the temple of Athena. I see this as Medusa's yielding to her instincts, to the realm of the unconscious. For this she drew the disapproval of Athena, the goddess born from her father's head rather than delivered by her mother. Medusa is body-centered, not head-centered. She may have been self-possessed, and like most self-possessed women, she was feared and punished for it.

Medusa was rendered seemingly impenetrable, representing that which is guarded by defenses that don't wish this instinctual nature to be seen or known. Her head writhes with snakes, reptilian instincts continuing to fuel this aspect of us that can't be denied if wholeness is to be achieved. This raging, wild thing is like what Jane Loevinger describes, "When salient experience must be unnoticed, disallowed, unacknowledged or forgotten, the result is incoherence in the self structure."[44]

---

[44] Siegel, D. J. (2012). *The Developing Mind: How Relationships and the Brain Interact to Shape Who We Are* (2nd ed.), p. 34. New York: Guilford Press.

We might compare Medusa, this raging, wild thing, to the ravages of trauma and the life of the amygdala, the seat of emotions and memory in the limbic brain. Overactivation in the brain may be triggered by circumstances in the present that tap into memories and pathways in the brain and body that cannot be looked upon or voiced. This is the incoherence and disruption that trauma victims live with in their daily lives.

Let's review the backstory: King Acrisus was a patriarchal figure willing to cast his daughter and grandson into the sea to preserve his own safety. The undervalued feminine was set adrift in the sea of unconsciousness.

This abandonment mirrors our collective consciousness, which continues to pursue patriarchal dominance over feminine values of relatedness, and nurturance. Then there is a shift in the grandson, Perseus, who so loves his mother that he's willing to risk his life on a fool's errand to protect her. Zeus supports his intent and sends help to assist the young hero in his effort.

There is little hope the wild creature can be slain without supernatural resources to assist. This is true as well in the supernatural effort required in the healing of narcissism.

Perseus has a helmet that renders him invisible. We might understand this as a dissolution of self-concept, replaced by the invisibility of simply being. In order to see an *other*, we have to stop looking only at ourselves. Forgetting self allows us to enter the field of resonance that exists between us.

Perseus has a mirror that allows him to see Medusa without looking at her directly. With Perseus invisible, only Medusa is reflected, creating an opening, a space in which she can be truly seen *as she is*, and there is a moment of oneness, a union in which transformative energies can enter.

This is like the I-Thou relationship described by Martin Buber. In the experience of relatedness, there is a loss of both I and Thou as we connect in the space of the hyphen. Buber is describing a field that includes the *whole being* of each object. In the myth, this occurs in the space of the mirror. With the mirror acting as the hyphen, the space of related-ness between Perseus and Medusa engenders a unity of being in that moment.

Perseus surrenders to invisibility, and his sword causes the surrender of Medusa. There is a state of joining in the moment of complete and coherent mirroring such that only oneness exists. A state of being develops in the brain/psyche, and the two systems amplify and co-regulate one another. According to Siegel, "Integration utilizes the resonance of different subsystems to achieve cohesive states and a coherent flow of states across time. Such a process creates a more complex, functionally linked system, which itself can become a subcomponent of even larger and more complex systems."[45]

This describes the transcendent function, the innate capacity in the human being to see without differentiation of parts, to see in wholes and therefore to become part of wholeness. In these moments, duality ceases and there is no separation but rather a joining and a state of oneness and wholeness.

Medusa symbolizes the unconscious and its contents. Llewellyn Vaughan-Lee writes, "Carl Jung wrote that the symbols of the unconscious place a great responsibility on the individual. If a symbol arises from the unconscious and is not consciously related to, it can turn inward and become devouring rather than creative.... The reflective stance of consciousness acts as a mediating mirror, like Perseus' shield, enabling us to work with the unconscious without being overwhelmed by its raw power. Without this mediating quality of consciousness, the psyche devours, or turns to stone, everything it encounters."[46]

Vaughan-Lee goes on to say, "Only individual consciousness can counter the pull of the unconsciousness. This is not a work that any religion, organization, or government can do. It is the individual hero who

---

[45] Siegel, D.J. (2012). *Developing Mind*, p. 322.
[46] Vaughan-Lee, L. (2007). *Alchemy of Light: Working with the Primal Energies of Life*, p. 85. Point Reyes Station, CA: Golden Sufi Center.

traditionally defeats the monster, symbolizing the role of our individual consciousness.... This is the responsibility of each of us."[47]

This is similar to Jung's statement, "The world hangs by a thin thread, and that thread is the psyche of man.... We are the great danger. The psyche is the great danger. What if something goes wrong with the psyche? And so it is demonstrated in our day what the power of the psyche is, how important it is to know something about it. But we know nothing."[48]

Something is wrong with the psyche, and we are tasked with its recovery. The encounter between Perseus and Medusa shows us a moment of recovery and what is needed for that to occur.

There is a falling away as both Perseus and Medusa surrender in their own ways and all that remains is a moment of pure reflection, a resonance, a joining, and in that moment something new emerges.

This is not unfamiliar. It is present in a numinous moment of gazing at the sky or a flower or the ocean, and in that moment of conscious experiencing, the self and that which it gazes upon both lose their boundaries. The individual feels a quality of joining with and becomes part of something larger than self.

---

[47] Vaughan-Lee, L. (2007). *Alchemy of Light*, p. 87.
[48] C.G. Jung interview, https://www.youtube.com/watch?v=ppFlVouq-Mc on 2019-3-30

The chaos of writhing snakes and the horrific visage of Medusa engaged in meeting the heroic, dynamic masculine that is able to see her truly, yields the emergence of a creature who has never before existed.

Eckhart Tolle speaks of a field of awareness that arises when we are in a state of presence. He says this state arising between two human beings is "the most essential factor in relationship on the new earth."[49] In other words, something new can emerge when this potent presence is allowed in the space between two people who are coherent in their connection.

In the myth, the mirror brings presence and the sword brings coherence to the encounter of Medusa and Perseus. The sword of the heroic masculine represents discernment and discrimination, like the Zen koan that describes "the knife that cuts things together."[50] The transcendent mirroring capacity allows the clear discrimination of what is self and what is not, and the discernment to know truth with certainty. With this blade, the shadow can be slain and its true nature revealed. Chrysaor and Pegasus emerge. A true warrior empowered and seated upon a winged horse, a vision of the true self

---

[49] Tolle, E. (2008). *A New Earth: Awakening to Your Life's Purpose*, p. 270. New York: Penguin Books.
[50] Author heard this Zen koan in a lecture by Marion Woodman.

that serves its own truth and values, carried by a spiritual creature, lifted by its own instincts.

What does it feel like to be seated on Pegasus, the winged horse? A. H. Almaas describes the return to the essential self: "There is a sense of newness and coolness, of lightness and lightheartedness, of the absence of burden and suffering, and presence of purity and peace. It is a nothingness, but it is a nothingness that is rich, that is satisfying precisely because of its emptiness.... It is the self experiencing itself *as* the infinity of peaceful space."[51]

In order to arrive here, Perseus must tolerate not knowing what to do. He must trust in truth and relinquish the ego and all its pursuits to align with the self. Then in the emptiness, one who says, "I am here now" may arise. This is the experience of pure being, of having a center of awareness separate from ego, but compassionate toward it. This becomes the new structure of the self.

It's like a child learning to walk. The child learns to walk and to talk without thinking, just following its instincts. Following the thread of self-inquiry, trusting instincts, reflecting the self and its shadow, a spontaneous unfolding can occur.

---

[51] Almaas, A. H. (2000). *Point of Existence*, p. 338.

"O this is the creature that does not exist.
They did not know that and in any case
—its motion, and its bearing, and its neck,
even to the light of its still gaze—they loved it.

Indeed it never *was*. Yet because they loved it,
a pure creature happened. They always
allowed room.
And in that room, clear, and left open,
it easily raised its head and scarcely needed
to be. They fed it with no grain, but ever
with the possibility that it might be.
And this gave the creature such strength.

It grew a horn out of its brow. One horn.
To a virgin it came hither white—
and was in the silver-mirror and in her.
—Rainer Marie Rilke, "Sonnets to Orpheus"

• • • •

# Chapter 7
# The Healing Journey

I am not I.
I am this one
Walking beside me whom I do not see,
Whom at time I manage to visit,
And at other times forget.
The one who remains silent when I talk,
The one who forgives, sweet, when I hate,
The one who takes a walk when I am indoors
The one who will remain standing when I die.

—Juan Ramón Jiménez[52]

We've been exploring narcissism and its wounds and following the thread of recovery through fairy tale and myths that inform the journey. Now we'll look at specific elements necessary for the transformation

---

[52] Jiménez, J. R. (1993). I am not I. In R. Bly, J. Hillman, & M. Meade, (Eds.). *The Rag and Bone Shop of the Heart: A Poetry Anthology.* New York: HarperCollins.

of narcissism and offer insight to explain how this might take place in the individual psyche.

When the psyche has been wounded, the ego takes up the space meant for the Self. The path of transformation begins by finding or creating space for the self. Even when the ego leaves not a breath of air for the self, believing the self continues to exist and that there is still space holding the self is necessary for recovery. Psyche always pursues conditions, circumstances, and opportunities to recover its wholeness.

At the beginning of a therapeutic process, the therapist holds space for the self. The therapist sees beyond the symptoms and personality structures to the pure being in the narrow sliver of space allowed by the ego.

For example, a woman comes into therapy with great anger toward her mother, and sees the problem as her anger. She has had a codependent relationship with her mother since she was fourteen, when her father passed away. She became caregiver for her mom, attempting to protect her from further pain and loss (an outcome far beyond her capacity to provide), and in the process, her own visibility was lost and her own needs set aside. Now her mother is ready to remarry and though the daughter is grown and has her own family, she is angry at the invisibility she feels as her mother invests all her energy in the new romance and again abandons her daughter's emotional experience. The space for the one who was abandoned at age fourteen, whose grief and needs were not seen, is held by the therapist to allow the depths of the self to begin to open.

All soul-searching activities, including therapy, painting, writing, dreaming, and meditation, are ways of seeking this space. Addiction and misguided pursuit of romantic interests are also efforts at soul-seeking.

In scripture it says, "I stand at the door and knock, if any hear my knock..."[53] I understand this as a reference to the abandoned or unseen aspects of Self/Soul that must continue to knock until it is heard.

At the beginning of the *Snow White* story, the queen hears a knock as she imagines the pure, snow-white innocence of a child. There is a space in imagination that holds this innocent child seeking birth. This is the way the psyche holds the true self, the soul in imagination containing the inner being until it can emerge.

Upon feeling the purity and innocence of the inner being, the queen pricks her finger and bleeds. Before we encounter the innocence at the center of the self, wounds stand at the threshold. It can be nearly impossible to see over or around the wounds to the innocence beyond.

---

[53] *Revelation* 3:20

When we only know our self as the ego, with all the constructed and defended aspects the ego employs to sustain itself, it's practically impossible to experience an *inner other*. This is what the queen is dreaming of as she imagines Snow White. It's what we mean we say, "I'm beside my self." It's the one Jimenez writes of in the poem that begins this chapter.

To get to this inner *other*, reflection is needed. Only what can be reflected can be seen. When the inner other is buried in the unconscious and the ego reigns supreme, even a glimpse is impossible. When ego says, "I am what I am," it's denying the inner duality of the self and the witness. Hearing and feeling this inner duality will in time enable us to open to the awareness of others.

In *Snow White*, the queen sits before an open window gazing at the pure white snow, a reflection of the possibility that this snow-white dimension exists in her. Sitting quietly, she glimpses an experience of otherness.

The woman who took care of her mother at age 14 feels a surge of anger, and that's not all. She also feels stirrings of the other, the one who has been lost and sad and wanting to be seen for a long time. Something is required to ignite a knock from the other, and in this case, it is feeling emotionally abandoned by mother again.

There are no lack of opportunities to hear the Self knocking, calling us toward otherness. Nature can call us to awareness of otherness. Music can open the heart to create a space to hear a greater other. Art can create a tremor of recognition. Empathy for another can help the door swing open. A sudden memory or insight can open the door to our own story.

Reflection, mirroring, is needed for us to know the pure snow-white expanse of ourselves and the deep, sad, longing within.

The narcissistic core lacks the capacity for reflection. To heal narcissistic wounds, outer reflection is needed to help us learn self-reflection. Witness the mirroring of a young child by her parents. The child yells, "Nooooo," when her way is thwarted and the parent reflects, "I know you're frustrated and disappointed." With this acknowledgment, the child can move to "Yes."

When there was no mirroring, it is as if one's affect and attributes have been painted black. There is a blank, a void.

A man came for therapy with a serious back injury that prevented him from continuing his work as a steel worker. His identity had been built around his strength and success constructing large buildings, moving beams, making his work tangible. He had been the strong man, the provider for his family, the best at his trade. Now he couldn't lift anything over twenty-five pounds. He was in a profound depression.

As we explored his history, I learned he'd had an overbearing and critical father. In the father's eyes, he couldn't do anything right. He dropped out of school and left home to save himself from further abuse.

Simultaneous with treatment for depression, he began a vocational rehabilitation program to learn new skills. He enrolled in a computer technology program and in each session with me he'd describe how overwhelmed he felt, incapable of learning new skills, he'd never be able to succeed.

Concerned about another possible failure for him, I consulted with his vocational counselor to get an assessment of his progress. When I described the man's concerns, the counselor took several minutes to be sure we were talking about the same person. She said he was doing extremely well in all performance aspects, and in fact he was the best student they'd ever had.

He had been unable to see that reflection in the dark mirror he was looking in; he saw only what his father had seen. There was no space for reflection of who he actually was. As I reflected to him the information I'd received and the excellence of his accomplishments, he was finally able to say, "I guess I'm not stupid," and he cried.

The last time I saw him, this blue-collar steel worker was wearing a white shirt and tie and was employed as a computer technology specialist in a successful company.

Narcissus helps us see that the transformative process does not stop at reflection. Reflection takes us to the threshold of the Self and leaves us there. The next step in the process of healing is difficult to bear.

Narcissus was entranced with the glimpse of the Self at this threshold, and in being thus captivated was unable to move and he died. He had no sense of where he was or what was happening, nor did he have the skills or resources to move forward. He was lost in the reflection of the Self.

Consider threshold experiences in your own life, the first day of school, starting a new job, graduation, marriage, illness, and the approach of death. All of these hold a numinous quality, each is celebrated with ritual and sacraments, because approaching the numinous without that kind of protection and support can, indeed, strike us dead.

The word *numinous* comes from the Latin *numen*, meaning a "deity or spirit presiding over a thing or space."[54] When we arrive at a threshold, we're at the precipice of stepping out of what or where or who we've been, the familiar, and into

---

[54] Wikipedia https://en.wikipedia.org/wiki/Numinous on 2019-3-30

what's new or next or not-yet-known. The crossing is mystery, and at the threshold we might feel terror or awe. This is an encounter with the unknown, the other.

Aldous Huxley describes it this way:

"The literature of religious experience abounds in references to the pains and terrors overwhelming those who have come, too suddenly, face-to-face with some manifestation of the *mysterium tremendum*. In theological language, this fear is due to the incompatibility between man's egotism and the divine purity, between man's self-aggravated separateness and the infinity of God."[55]

At the threshold of an encounter with the Self, we find ourselves small and vulnerable, and the other—the mystery, the unknown—as awesome and overwhelmingly separate. Narcissus experiences this numinosity when he glimpses the beautiful reflection of Self in the water. He can see it, but he cannot touch it; he can pursue it, but it eludes him; he can perceive its depths but he cannot grasp them; he can yearn for it, but he cannot possess it. This is a reflection of the Self which is outside the self, something Narcissus has never experienced before. To glimpse the Self is a numinous experience. Nar-

---

[55] Huxley, A. (2004). *The Doors of Perception and Heaven and Hell*, p. 55. New York: HarperCollins.

cissus fell in love with its reflection and was overcome by it.

The term *numinous* was popularized by Rudolf Otto, a German theologian, who explained it as "non-rational, non-sensory experience or feeling whose primary and immediate object is outside the self."[56] He was describing this kind of encounter with something "wholly other."

Imagine an encounter like this. Perhaps you encounter a deer in the woods in the clearing ahead of you. First you feel surprise, then a tremble of fear, and finally a sense of awe and curiosity. The deer is still, eating leaves from the bush, and you grow still as well, observing and experiencing the other in this moment. You hesitate to move or even breathe, as any sound might disturb the encounter and cause the deer to flee. This is a numinous experience.

What if it had been a bear rather than a deer. You'd probably feel terror, and instead of standing still you might panic and back away to get as much distance and safety from this other as you can. This, too, is a numinous encounter, but of a different quality, one you fear and wish to avoid.

Either or both of these experiences occur when you encounter the Self. Narcissus glimpsed beauty, depth, and otherness and wanted to know

---

[56] Otto, R. (1923). *The Idea of the Holy.* New York: Oxford University Press.

more. But suppose instead of beauty he had encountered the face of a terrified child or a reflection of rage so deep it threatens to explode. Would he have recoiled?

A threshold experience can be overwhelming. The body may be unprepared for the terror and vulnerability that arise. I remember my daughter's first day of kindergarten. We prepared with a visit to the school, reading books and talking about feelings. Still, when the big yellow bus pulled up in front of our house and it was empty because she was the first to be picked up, she threw herself on me, tears flowing, clasping with arms and legs to the secure other that was known rather than moving toward this daunting, empty, unknown other that was about to consume her. I peeled her off and placed her on the bus. The world was waiting for her. I paced and drank too much coffee during the few hours she was away. And then she came home smiling.

Terror stands at the threshold. We don't know if we can do it. We have no idea what awaits. We're not sure we have the inner resources that are needed. The most difficult question we face when we turn toward the Self is, what if there's nothing there, or what if it's hideous, unbearable, or broken? The narcissist prefers the known, the inflated ego, over an encounter with a self that might burst the bubble, disappoint, or cause intolerable vulnerability.

Thresholds require preparation. We must have insight into where we stand and what we're moving toward. Rituals and sacraments need protocols, containers to hold the numinous and unfamiliar, and language to describe the experience. There's comfort knowing there will be markers and resources along the way. With this security, we might be able to gaze at what's there and dare enter into an encounter with the other.

But no matter how prepared we might be, at the threshold we'll be gazing into a void; this is the next element of the transformative experience. The void is absolutely unknown, and so there's an apparent emptiness and darkness to it. The void is all potential. We've entered a dimension beyond form. From the threshold, the void appears dark and empty. We have not yet ventured forth to discover what's actually there.

We hear the words, "I pronounce you husband and wife," and we are standing at the threshold of the void. We know the experiences of romance, coupling, relationship, and now wedding. But we have no idea what marriage will be. We might have noble, naïve, romantic notions of happily ever after, but we have not yet encountered the challenges and ongoing demands of marriage. A void morphs into form one moment at a time, calling forth all the potentials and resources needed to create something new, something that has never existed before.

Calling forth a new thing that has never existed before takes us toward Medusa and her story. She guides us on the final steps of the path of transformation as she teaches us exactly what's needed to see into the void, to tolerate that great unknowing and move into the creative process that will bring forth something that has never existed before.

Medusa is a perfect metaphor for void. She is dark, scary, and unknowable. She appears to be a fierce power, and we don't know what dangers may lurk. There are the snakes writhing on her head! This is the primitive, instinctual level of being. If we are not in the primitive, instinctual level of being, we are not in the void.

Being mindful of the experience of entering the void, we can focus on the body. We can tune in to the visceral, somatic, physiological experience that stands at the entry to the void. Adrenaline pumps terror through our body. Our heart pounds and our palms sweat. Our body feels as though it's about to fly apart into pieces. There may be a sensation of falling, of descent.

The only task at this moment is to stay, to stay with the experience. Usually when a visceral experience becomes terrifying, we run. Can we stay? Can we simply be? This is why Perseus is carrying the mirror rather than looking directly at Medusa. A look into her dark eyes, her writhing snake-headed presence would be too activating, too alarming to stay present. Perseus's clear mirror allows him to see and to stay, and in that moment of pure seeing and staying, he is able to behead the void.

When people describe the experience of falling into the void, it usually begins with terror and the desire to flee, the wish to be rescued, the impulse to find a way out. But if we stay, just beyond the terror is a shift. Suddenly, there is an experience that is new. This is the next transformative element: *only experience*.

When falling into a void, there's no time for thought, effort, or motive. Time and space fall away, and there is only now and this, only the phenomenological—that which is occurring in the moment. This is the moment of *emergence*, which is the next element of transformation.

In the phenomenal experience of surrendering to the void, there comes what is sometimes described as a soft landing, a friendly darkness, love instead of death. Only by yielding to the field of awareness, which is simply experiencing, can something new emerge. In this moment, the brain and psyche are completely plastic, malleable, open. A resonance, a joining with what occurs, and an altered state of being are experienced. In that moment, Perseus sees the reflection of Medusa and she sees him, and both are fully engaged in the experience. It is a moment of unexpected, visceral joining.

Yes, it's a mystery, but one you are familiar with. It's the last orgasm you had; it's standing on the sand at the edge of the ocean where you merge with sea and sky; it's gazing into the eyes of your newborn child and recognizing that all is one.

Emergence is the birth of something new at the moment we surrender to experience, to what is. This transcendent hope is Pegasus, the winged horse emerging from the void, the pure power of the instinct-driven creature in all its glory, with wings that will lift you up and carry you even further. Pegasus is the end of longing, the union of matter and spirit, our human and divine natures coming together. This is possible in the moment of emergence, because in surrendering to the experience of the void, we enter the realm of nonduality beyond horse or angelic creature to the both/and nature of a winged horse. In this field of awareness, either/or stops.

This is the field where all comes together. We can call it relatedness. We finally know our self as the one greater than the sum of our parts. It is the moment when self returns to its innocent wholeness and is raised into a new form. It is the end of narcissism (which divides and separates) and the return to Self as a whole, the emergence of the transcendent function.

The process of transformation would seem to end gloriously in this emergence, but this is not the end. That only happens in fairy tales. This state of awareness, this new creature requires integration into our being, and into the world. In a moment of pure reflection, Medusa is slain. But the human psyche needs to process all this in an ongoing fashion during diverse states of being. We cannot hold that glorious moment of becoming a new creature, but we can, with practice, try to bring it more and more into our daily life.

Because this is a phenomenon and not a structure, we will have to learn to clear the space, let go of the obstructions, and feel into the field of awareness we have now experienced. Moments of union occur at the end of every exhale, but awareness and effort are needed for this to resonate in our very physiology.

What does persist is the remembering, literally *re-membering*. Once we've had the experience of emerging oneness, it's a visceral, living, organic experience of what lies past the terror. We remember the soft landing, the numinous joining that contains the love, grace, innocence, and presence. It is our experience, and remembering it becomes a doorway to reentry. All practices going forward can originate from that organic experience of coherence, resonance, wholeness. This union is the final element of transformation, a sense of union within and a sense of union without. There is no duality within when in the field of awareness of what simply is. We are now in being. There is no duality without when we surrender to what is, as separateness falls away and there is simply I Am That.

Consider the essence of the transformation process Snow White, Narcissus, and Medusa have shown us, and see how this may unfold in your own experience:

Space
Reflection
Threshold
Void
Experience
Emergence
Integration
Union

• • • •

# Chapter 8
# Inner Work

In this chapter, I want to offer guidance for entering the path of self-inquiry, or self-reflection. Transformation is experiential, not just something to read or think about it, although these might be helpful preliminary steps.

When the capacity for self-reflection constellates, our ability to observe what's present increases. Therapist and teacher Radmila Moacanin describes her own experience on the path of self-discovery: "The art of letting things happen, action through inaction, letting go of oneself as told by Meister Eckhart, became for me the key that opens the door to the way. *We must let things happen in the psyche.* For us, this is an art of which most people know nothing. Consciousness is forever interfering, helping, correcting, and negating, never leaving the psychic process to grow in peace."[57] She describes how this

---

[57] Moacanin, R. (2002). *The Essence of Jung's Psychology and Tibetan*

letting go and letting be process allows the unconscious to "fertilize" consciousness, and consciousness
to "illuminate" unconsciousness.

As one undertakes this path and this process,
an integration is occurring that is the deconstruction
of former ways of being directed by the ego, and a
new way of being, the way of the self, emerges. "The
ego that has developed in response to the pressures
and dictates of the outer world, and the cultural
environment, at this point bows and gives way to the
pressures and urges of the individual's inner world,
his inner being, his soul, the Self."[58] If one is to
achieve the depths of self-realization and connection
to the numinous, letting go is necessary.

All of Jung's work on individuation grew out
of his own inner work. He took to heart Socrates'
advice to Know Thyself. Jung describes how he set
aside time to be outdoors and play in the sand
creating mandalas. He kept journals to record his
dreams and his experiences in active imagination.
His art and his work carving stones and building
were profound expressions of the experiences of
self-discovery. His journal and artwork were published
in 2009 as *The Red Book*. Near the beginning of the
book, he says,

---

*Buddhism: Western and Eastern Paths to the Heart*, p. 44, emphasis
added. Somerville, MA: Wisdom Publications.
[58] ibid.

"When I had the vision of the flood in October of the year 1913, it happened at a time that was significant for me as a man. At that time, in the fortieth year of my life, I had achieved honor, power, wealth, knowledge and every human happiness. Then my desire for the increase of these trappings ceased, the desire ebbed from me and horror came over me. The vision of the flood seized me and I felt the spirit of the depths, but I did not understand him. Yet he drove me on with unbearable inner longing and I said: My soul, where are you? Do you hear me? I speak, I call to you—are you there? I have returned. I am here again. I have shaken the dust of all the lands from my feet, and I have come to you.'"[59]

Jung then began a process of engaging with his own unconscious and experienced the process of individuation. All of his prolific writing and teaching grew out of this internal, self-discovery process. He felt as though he was going crazy, and from the outside looking in, it does look and sound like someone coming undone. Instead, he found his own story, his own inner map, his own recovery of the true self. He then spent the rest of his life writing, teaching and treating patients so they might also discover what he came to call *The Way*.

---

[59] Jung, C.G. (2009). *The Red Book* (pp. 231-232).

After reading about Jung's practices for self-discovery, I adopted many of his methods in my own inner work. I've kept journals since I was a young girl. The journal has often been the mirror I needed when that was lacking from other sources. I could see and hear the voice of the one who was writing on the page. It was not always someone I was familiar with. The words, emotions, needs, and images often would surprise me. As an adult in the midst of my own times of soul searching, the journal became a place to explore listening deeply to my inner experience, to express archetypal energies that were larger than I could hold, to dialogue with my self and with God. In these pages, I could rant or grieve or go on a vision quest. This place of private reflection has served me well.

There are things, however, that words cannot hold. Again using Jung's model, I took to keeping paper on which I had drawn a circle handy. Then when a feeling or an image seemed to need expression, I would place it in the circle. Jung calls the mandala an archetype. It lives in the psyche as a symbol of the Self; and he drew beautiful mandalas representing moments and characters significant to his own individuation process. When we approach the unconscious with no preconceived notions and suspended judgment, the unconscious will offer some expression of what is being felt, of what needs to be seen, and again, we have a mirror for reflecting aspects of the self. My work is primitive; you don't have to be an artist to use this technique. Lines and colors, even images I've cut from magazines express something at work in the psyche and give me a tangible experience of it.

There are times when the feelings or energies needing attention are too large to fit on paper. These might require movement, dance, drumming, or even running or screaming. The body needs to be allowed to feel and express what is moving from the unconscious into consciousness. It's important to engage with what is seeking expression in a way that offers safety and containment. It can be helpful to take part in experiential groups or retreats where space is made for this. Or try having a witness you trust to support your process.

Attending to dreams is another valuable practice. Jung's work in this realm is very valuable. It can be helpful to read about dreamwork and/or find someone experienced to assist you in exploring your dreams. Dreams can be life-changing. The most profound period of my own process of growth and self-realization began with a dream. There have been dreams and dream figures all along the way for me that have pointed to aspects of consciousness calling for attention, and dreams that integrate changes that were occurring into the psyche. By keeping a dream journal, drawing dream images, and dialoging with characters in the dream, your conscious standpoint will forge a deeper relationship with the unconscious. There can be dramatic awakenings through the dream, and there can also be great comfort in being accompanied by the dream's characters and stories. From the Jungian perspective, dreams are a field of living, archetypal energies that are making their presence known. Engaging with the dream material as you would engage in dialogue with another can bring profound insight and experiential change.

Active imagination is an extension of dreaming, bringing dreamlike imagery or continuing dreams that came while you were asleep into your waking life. You allow the mind to open to imagination, and trust what occurs. If a new figure shows up in a dream or if you're not sure what's being asked of you, engage in an imaginary dialogue between the dreamer and the figure in the dream. You can ask questions and listen for and visualize answers.

Jung spoke of the need to discover our own myth. Snow White, Narcissus, and Medusa have told us their stories, now it is time to discover your own, your life story told from the perspective of your soul. It is beyond the details like where you were born or how many siblings you had, to the wounds you've experienced and the meaning and purpose your soul may find in that.

There's an Alcoholics Anonymous saying: "No one can do it for you, and you can't do it alone." That certainly applies here. Many have walked and continue to walk this path of seeking greater consciousness and learning to embody the self. Use the resources you're drawn to, because guidance and support are really necessary. A therapist who can offer the mirroring and containing space you need can be an excellent source of support. I've also seen this work done by groups of people coming together to explore and support one another. A group can create a powerful experiential field in which the sum of the parts is unimaginably greater than any individual. Other sources of community, such as church groups, dream groups, meditation groups, or classes, can also be sources of support. And there are books, poetry, music, and art that may call to you with words and images that are just what you need. Jung was attentive to synchronicities like the book that just falls off the shelf and holds the answer you didn't even know you needed. The Self is seeking you; you are not alone.

• • • •

## Chapter 9
# The Return

*"Now you see through a mirror darkly, what then you shall see face to face."*

—Corinthians 13

*"The end of all our exploring will be to arrive where we started and know the place for the first time."*

—T.S. Eliot[60]

We've been looking at the self mostly through the lenses of psychology and neurobiology. But the story of the self cannot be complete without also looking through the lens of spirituality.

For someone with extreme narcissistic wounding, there are no real others, and that includes an absence of the Great Other, or God. An encounter with the

---

[60] Eliot, T.S. (1968). *Four Quartets*, Section V., p. 47. Boston: Mariner Books.

divine is not possible for the narcissist, nor is I-Thou relatedness.

Jung saw the divine as an archetype, one that is always with us. He was clear that the work of individuation is a path of return in which the soul is redeemed and a connection to God becomes known. All spiritual traditions teach, in their own ways, that the task of self-discovery is the task of discovering the God within.

We cannot complete our journey into the personal shadow and the collective unconscious without describing the encounter with the divine. We will have failed to make the whole journey if we cannot be brave enough to look into this deepest, most awesome aspect of our being.

So far, we have considered the changes in the psychological structures of the relationship between the ego and the self, between consciousness and the unconscious, and the expanding capacity of the self as it integrates its true nature. We will not have seen all the way to the bottom of the pool in which Narcissus is gazing if we don't examine the potential, the source, from which the self arises. Beyond the personal level of the self are the collective and transpersonal levels. It is this grandeur that makes individuation a daunting, lifelong project. However, it also this recognition that offers hope for the transformation of narcissism.

In the depths of the self we discover that, at our roots, our uniqueness falls away and there is a universal pattern from which our self-expression arises. In Hinduism, these are named Brahmin, the absolute, and Atman, the individual expression or manifestation in human form. Brahmin is the form-less, creative principle behind all that is manifested in the form of created beings. Atman is the personal expression of this creative principle in form.

In Christianity the presence of the indwelling spirit, which is the image of God, is also recognized as the true nature of the self. Thomas Merton explains:

"In Christianity the inner self is simply a stepping stone to an awareness of God. Man is the image of God, and his inner self is a kind of mirror in which God not only sees Himself, but reveals Himself to the "mirror" in which He is reflected. Thus, through the dark, transparent mystery of our own inner being we can, as it were, see God 'through a glass.' All of this is of course pure metaphor. It is a way of saying that our being somehow commu-nicates directly with the Being of God, Who is in us. If we enter into ourselves, find our true self, and then pass 'beyond' the inner 'I,' we sail forth into the immense darkness in which we confront the 'I AM' of the Almighty."[61]

Through the individuation process, we have been developing our capacity to be the mirror. Once capable of mirroring, we can engage in the practice of mindfulness, neutral observing, and meditation. As we become mindful, observing moves from something we're doing to something we are. The move from mindfulness to *being observing* opens the threshold to consciousness, pure awareness, simply being. As the silent witness, we can glimpse the unmanifest, the all being, that which exists before any expression of the many phenomena of expression. Almaas says that the silent witness allows observation of "a vast expanse underlying the process of continual creation."[62] In that space, "we experience a stillness beyond all stillness, an absolute and total stillness, a condition prior to all manifestation, movement, and change. We experience ourselves as a vastness, an immensity, an expanse so deep it is absolutely dark. Though dark and still, inscrutable and silent, it is the source of all luminosity and light…. The light is the unfolding logos, whose pattern is the totality of existence."[63]

---

[61] Merton, T. (1992). The inner experience. In L. S. Cunningham (Ed.). *Thomas Merton: Spiritual Master,* p. 302. Mahwah, NJ: Paulist Press.
[62] Almaas, A.H. (2004). *The Inner Journey Home: The Soul's Realization of the Unity of Reality* (p. 377). Boulder, CO: Shambhala.
[63] ibid., p. 378.

This teaching is sometimes called the wisdom tradition or perennial tradition, because it appears across time, cultures, and faith traditions. Eknath Easwaran describes *four aspects of this wisdom tradition* as expressed by Meister Eckhart that correlates with what we've been exploring in our fairy tale and myths.[64] The first is that there is a light in the soul that is uncreated and uncreatable. In *Snow White*, we saw this in the form of pure white snow, the innocence at the core of the self at birth, seen as divine in spiritual traditions. We can understand its divinity as its unconstructed nature. It is not man-made. Its essence is from an unknown source.

The second aspect of the perennial tradition is that this core, the divine essence, can be realized. For it to be realized, it must be discovered and not hidden under the personality. Though the pure nature at the core has been wounded, it's still there and can be consciously embodied. Snow White slept, but she wasn't dead. Narcissus discovered in the image reflected in the pool a self he'd never seen before, that moved him with such power he merged with it.

Meister Eckhart says discovering this divine essence is life's highest goal. Our life's meaning and

---

[64] Rohr, R. daily meditation 1/29/2018, quoting Eknath Easwaran. (1966). *Original Goodness: On the Beatitudes of the Sermon on the Mount* (pp. 8-9). Tomales, CA: Nilgiri Press.

purpose is not in the pursuit of possessions that might satisfy the ego, but in the discovery and recovery of the divine center within. The way to this inner divine center is what Jung describes as the process of individuation in *The Red Book* and later called *The Way*. Christ said, "I am the way, the truth and the life." He is offering himself as a model for the way to return to the divine.

To discover The Way, we have to go beyond Narcissus's glimpse of the Self into the encounter with Medusa, where we can be transformed into a new being that embodies the redeemed, divine core. Everyone who has a conversion experience, such as being born again, speaks of the visceral magnitude of that deconstruction and rebirthing. There is often a terrifying vulnerability and surrender, followed by the emergence of what feels like a new being.

The last aspect of this wisdom tradition is the recognition that the divinity we discover at the core of the Self exists in one and all. We come to know not only the wholeness and holiness within the self, but the Self as part of all creation.

A client recently shared a dream that expressed the reunion with the divine core at the heart of the Self. He had struggled for years with the severe neglect and abuse he experienced as a child. He drowned his sorrow with alcohol because of the unbearable pain. He lost a son several years ago and has been working through that tremendous grief. In his current work, he is finally facing directly into his aloneness, learning to bear the darkness that dwells there, and acknowledging the innocent child within. He gave me permission to share this dream:

"I'm in a dimly lit, run-down room. The wallpaper is a faded, grayish flower pattern. I notice that there's someone in the room with me, and I turn around and see a shabbily dressed man about my age leaning against the wall next to the door. He looks like a homeless bagman. I ask him who he is, and he replies, 'I am your True Self.'

"I say back to him that he looks so shabbily dressed, and he replies that I haven't been taking very good care of him. He tells me that I abandoned him, but he has never abandoned me. I ask him who my True Self is, and he replies that the True Self is the soul's individual emanation of the love and grace of Christ. I ask him how would I know if what he is saying is true. He tells me that I can never know. I can only feel it.

"So, I ask him how I can I feel it, and he says, I'll let you feel this. Inside of me, this hobo transforms into a magnificent specimen of radiant beauty, and my entire being becomes filled with the love and grace of Christ. I know what this is, because I experienced it with my son when he died. The White Light had come to reside inside of me. My soul was imbued with Divine Love, the Love of Christ, the Grace of Christ.

"All of this took place without words, just as it had during my time with my son. The void I have been trying to fill with alcohol and other compulsive behaviors was filled beyond overflowing....

"I woke up at 1:30 in the morning and I was just crying. I knew I had been transformed and that I was never going to be the same from that moment forward. I forgave everybody. Most important, I forgave myself. I let go of my story. At long last, at age 70, I'd come home to myself, to my lost self, to my True Self."

These moments of return, of self-realization, transform the narcissistic wounds we have carried for a lifetime. In this example, my client's greatest fear had been of his failure and financial ruin. Though he's a very intelligent, capable, and professional, his parents had told him he "would never amount to anything," and that had been his core fear until this dream. Now the hobo he was most afraid of revealed his true nature as divine, and this man is finally at home.

Human beings have a need, motivation, and capability to pursue our return home. The world desperately needs this to restore the unity and relatedness that is the true nature of the world. "Each particular being in the universe is needed by the entire universe. With this understanding of our profound kinship with all life, we can establish the basis for a flourishing Earth community."[65] Our transformation of narcissism and the return to the self are not for our personal benefit alone. They also serve the collective, of which we are a part.

Individuation restores the split between ego and self, consciousness and the unconscious, self and others, self and God. The conclusion of all our effort is to discover the nonduality that exists in all. Theologian Paul Tillich shared with Jung the understanding that "man's sense of the divine arises from within."[66] Tillich and Jung saw the presence of God in "human experience from the dawn of self consciousness," leading man to greater conscious-ness.[67] They saw God as continually moving man toward increasing self-transcendence and greater unity within and with all that is. Jung saw God as residing in the collective unconscious. Tillich affirmed God as the ground of being and therefore the self as capable of discovering the "experience and reality of God" in his own interior.[68]

---

[65] Berry, T. (2006). *Evening Thoughts: Reflecting on Earth as Sacred Community*. M. E. Tucker (Ed.) (pp. 57-58, 62). San Francisco: Sierra Club Books. As quoted in Richard Rohr 2018-2-21.

[66] Dourley, J. (1981). *The Psyche as Sacrament: A Comparative Study of C.G. Jung and Paul Tillich* (p. 9). Toronto: Inner City Books.

[67] ibid., p. 10.

[68] ibid., p. 20.

The ground of being, God, as the source is the very bottom of the pool in which Narcissus gazes, and in that moment of contact with the numinous, Narcissus is overwhelmed. To see God, and be seen by God, is to know our true self. This glimpse of the divine is the beginning of the deconstruction of the sense of self, an essential step in the healing of narcissism. As long as the separate self-structure exists, we experience alienation from our self, from others and from the natural world. It took Perseus and Medusa to demonstrate that a transformational encounter that brings forth a new being can occur.

The gods equipped Perseus with invisibility, the deconstruction of the self-concept. They gave him a reflecting mirror that allowed him to tolerate the immense energy of darkness. He had the knife of discernment and discrimination to slice through the last remnants of constructed being to reveal the true nature within. It's then that Pegasus is born, pure white and winged, the symbol of embodied spirit. Pegasus offers us the formless purity which is at the center restored to its true nature. This is the healing potential that lies within each of us. When Medusa is slain, she surrenders her constructed form and becomes "a completely new dimension, a dimension that emphasizes not the object—yourself as body, senses, and mind—but emphasizes the light."[69]

---

[69] Klein, J. (n.d.). I Am. Quoted in Richard Miller, *Manual 1: iRest*

Narcissism mends in self-realization. When we know the self as a part of the whole, related to and interconnected with all that is, we can live as creative potential manifesting in form, and bring light, compassion, warmth, relatedness, and mercy to the world. This realization lives in the collective unconscious. In our commitment to self-discovery, we help bring forth self- realization in the collective.

*Yoga Nidra*, p. 156. Sebastopol, CA: Anahata Press.

• • • •

# Epilogue

Ignorance allows evil to persist, and narcissism is an evil that impedes our individual and collective potential. Exploring my own wounding has motivated the study of narcissism for many years. The world's current suffering led me to write this book.

It's my hope that it offers some clarity and insight into understanding narcissism. I hope it also reveals that there is a path, a way, to release us from the grip of narcissism. We live in discouraging times. When we look at the current American government and other close-minded regimes and followers world-wide, at violence and abuses of power becoming normalized, becoming more enlightened about narcissism's darkness and its healing is an important element in addressing the issues before us. There is still hope of self-realization by millions pursuing the journey of self-recovery.

I have spent more than 40 years offering psy-chotherapy, and I can tell you of the beauty that lies within. Psyche knows the way to our full potential if we will only yield to her direction. She is bringing

us home to the Beloved. In *The Radiance Sutras,*
meditation teacher Lorin Roche translates for us the
ancient *Vijnana Bhairava Tantra,* which is a conver-
sation between the God, the creative power of the
universe, and the Goddess, the consciousness that
permeates everywhere. The Goddess begins the con-
versation with an inquiry:

> "Beloved and radiant lord of the space before
> birth,
> Revealer of essence,
> Slayer of the ignorance that binds us,
>
> You who in play have created this universe
> And permeated all forms in it
> With never-ending truth
> I have been wondering…
>
> I have been listening to the hymns of creation,
> Enchanted by the verses,
> Yet still I am curious.
>
> What is this delight-filled universe
> Into which we find ourselves born?
> What is this mysterious awareness
> Shimmering everywhere within it?"

Soon the God takes up her inquiry and
responds,

"Beloved, your questions
Touch the heart of wonder,
The path of intimacy with all of life—
Weaving together body and soul,
Sex and spirit, individuality and universality.

This is my Cave of Secrets.
Your inquiry has led you here.
I feel your fingers on my pulse.

Come with me.
Leave behind everything you know.
The teachings about me are
A light show put on by the celestial musicians,
As beautiful and insubstantial as clouds.

Elaborate rituals and garish images
May be useful in meditation when your mind is
whirling with thoughts
Of sex, money, and power, wandering like an
elephant in heat.
Go ahead and use these tools, yet know,
Beating drums and blaring trumpets
Cannot summon the One who is already present.

I am not a collection of incantations
Known only to experts.
I am not a ladder to be climbed,
A sequence for piercing energy centers in your
body.
I am not to be found at the end of a long road.
I am right here."[70]

---

[70] Roche, L. (2014). *The Radiance Sutras: 112 Gateways to the Yoga of Wonder and Delight* (pp. 15, 21-23). Boulder, CO: Sounds True.

• • • •

# Acknowledgments

I want to thank all those who have helped bring this book to life. I am deeply grateful for the many clients with whom I've had the privilege to work—and without whom I would not be who I am, nor would I have been able to collect and offer the wisdom located here.

I appreciate the support and encouragement of my earliest readers, Jim Gach and Kim Yamas. Thank you for your generous offering of time and your suggestions which enhanced my effort. Thank you also to my friends and colleagues who have had confidence in the project and cheered me on. I was very fortunate to find a very experienced and capable editor, Arnie Kotler. Thank you, Arnie; you saw what was needed to make the book more accessible to the reader and allow me to say what I intended. I will always be grateful for your patient editing and support in this process of writing my first book.

I am especially thankful for my children, Rachel and Clark. They make brief appearances in the book in some stories, but if the whole story were told, they are where I've learned everything essential to know. I love you always. Thank you to my husband, Gordon, who offered encouragement and support as I spent many, many hours in the basement writing.

And thank you, dear reader, for seeking the Self; all who seek shall find.

# Glossary

**active imagination:** a practice recommended by Jung for working with dreams and archetypes. Imagination is used to have a dialogue with a dream figure, to imagine the next scene in a dream, or other such things as usual thinking and judgment are suspended.

**ego:** the self-concept constructed through experience and culture. The ego is a necessary organizing principle in the psyche for functioning in the world. When wounded, it pursues its own interests. In its healthy nature, it is a vehicle for action and decision in the world on behalf of the Self.

**experiential self:** the core of the self which actually experiences life, including thoughts, feelings, sensation, and will, the essence of being.

**I-ness:** one's felt sense of being; a sense of being a separate self.

**individuation:** an internal process in the psyche which is an expanding consciousness of aspects of the self and the integration of these aspects into a larger sense of Self.

**mandala:** artwork done in the form of a circle and was considered by Jung as a symbol of the Self.

**mindfulness:** the capacity to observe one's own experience including sensation, emotion, and thought.

**persona:** the presentation of self as it appears to others in the world; one's image or face in the world as directed by the ego.

**Self:** the conscious and unconscious aspects of being, an archetype of the wholeness of human being, including the transpersonal aspect of consciousness; the God within.

**self:** conscious aspects of being including mind, emotions, sensation, and body. An organizing principle at the center of being.

**self-discovery:** consciousness or realization of aspects of one's true nature.

**self-reflection:** the ability to observe, contemplate, perceive the self; a level of consciousness capable of internal mirroring or witnessing.

**Soul:** the immaterial or spiritual essence of the human being; the animating essence of the self.

**true self:** the essence of the self, free of the persona and ego; the unconstructed self, not man-made.

**vijnyanamya kosha:** a level of consciousness that is neutral; the capacity of conscious non-judging witnessing, sometimes called witness consciousness.

• • • •

# Bibliography

Ackerman, D. (2004). *An Alchemy of Mind*. New York: Scribner.

Almass, A.H. (1996). *The Point of Existence: Transformation of Narcissism in Self-Realization*. Berkeley, California: Diamond Books.

Almaas, A.H. (2004). *The Inner Journey Home: Soul's Realization of the Unity of Reality*. Boston & London: Shambhala Publications.

Conforti, M. (2003). *Field, Fate and Form: Patterns in Mind, Nature, & Psyche*. New Orleans: Spring Journal Books.

Cruz, L. & Buser, S. (2016). *A Clear and Present Danger: Narcissism in the Era of Donald Trump*. Asheville, NC: Chiron Publications.

Dourley, J. P. (1981). *The Psyche as Sacrament: A Comparative Study of C.G. Jung and Paul Tillich*. Toronto: Inner City Books.

Hamilton, A. J. (2009). Neurons of compassion. *Spirituality & Health*, Sept./Oct.

Helminski, K. E. (1992). *Living Presence: A Sufi Way to Mindfulness & the Essential Self*. New York: Penguin Putnam, Inc.

Jung, C.G. (2009). *The Red Book, Liber Novus*. New York: W.W. Norton and Company.

Kiesling, S. (2006). Wired for compassion. *Spirituality and Health*, Sept./Oct.

Kunitz, S. & Lentine, G. (2005). *The Wild Braid*. New York: W.W. Norton and Company.

Miller, R. *Training Manual I for iRest Yoga Nidra*.

Moacanin, R. (2003). *The Essence of Jung's Psychology and Tibetan Buddhism*. Boston: Wisdom Publications.

Perluss, B. (2006). Touching earth, finding spirit: A passage into the symbolic landscape. *Spring Journal* 76, Psyche and Nature. New Orleans: Fall.

Prendergast, J. J., Fenner, P., Krystal, S. (Eds.). (2003). *The Sacred Mirror*. St. Paul, Minnesota: Paragon House.

Ray, R. A. (2008). *Touching Enlightenment: Finding Realization in the Body*. Boulder, Colorado: Sounds True.

Roche, L. (2014). *The Radiance Sutras*. Boulder, Colorado: Sounds True.

Schwartz-Salant, N. (1982). *Narcissism and Character Transformation: The Psychology of Narcissistic Character Disorders*. Toronto, Canada: Inner City Books.

Siegel, D. (2010). *Mindsight: The New Science of Personal Transformation*. New York: Bantam.

Siegel, D. (2003). *Parenting From the Inside Out*. New York: Tarcher/Putnam.

Sullivan, B. (2013). *Psychotherapy Grounded in the Feminine Principle*. Asheville, NC: Chiron Publications.

Tolle, E. (2005). *A New Earth: Awakening to Your Life's Purpose*. New York: Plume Publisher.

Vaughan-Lee, L. (2007). *Alchemy of Light*. Inverness, CA: The Golden Sufi Center.

● ● ● ●

# Credits

With gratitude to the following for permission to print previously published material:

Rumi, excerpt from "The Inner Garment of Love," translated by Kabir Helminski, from *The Rumi Collection*, edited by Kabir Helminski. Copyright ©1998 by Kabir Helminski. Reprinted by arrangement with The Permissions Company LLC on behalf of Shambhala Publications Inc., Boston, MA. www.shambhala.com

Excerpt from "Your Mysterious Giving," translated by Kabir Helminski, from *The Pocket Rumi*, © 2001 by Kabir Edmund Helminski. Reprinted by arrangement with The Permissions Company LLC on behalf of Shambhala Publications Inc., Boston, MA. www.shambhala.com

Excerpts from A. H. Almaas, *The Point of Existence: Transformations of Narcissism in Self-Realizations*. Copyright © 1987 by A-Hameed Ali. Published by arrangement with Diamond Books. Reprinted by arrangement with The Permissions Company LLC on

●  ●  ●  ●

# About the Author

 Gayle Bohlman, LCSW-C, has offered therapeutic relationship for clients since 1980. At the essence of her work are presence, supporting the striving toward wholeness as the psyche seeks itself, accurate mirroring of the Self, and a related and integrative process for accessing mind, body, and spirit in the work of healing and becoming one's self. In her work with clients, Gayle makes use of cognitive behavioral therapy, Jungian principles, Eye Movement Desensitization and Reprocessing (EMDR), body-centered psychotherapy, yoga, iRest yoga nidra meditation, and Imago marital therapy. Her expertise has proven helpful for clients experiencing depression, anxiety, trauma, life transitions, relationship problems, and greater spiritual development. She lives and works outside of Baltimore, Maryland.